Getting Acquainted with the Bible

ITS MAKEUP, PURPOSE, AND STORY

To Caroline,

In gratitude for your support. Grace & peace.

David Anguish

David Anguish

5 | 30 | 19

CarChlex Books

Searcy, AR

CarChlex Books
1210 North Main Street
Searcy, AR 72143
www.davidanguish.com

Book Layout ©2017 BookDesignTemplates.com

Cover Design by Kenneth Mills

Getting Acquainted with the Bible/ David Anguish. —1st ed.

ISBN 978-0-578-43427-8

For my grandchildren, Chloe and Alex,
in memory of their Gamma,
in the hope that they will seek the Word
as diligently as she did.

Teach me, O LORD, the way of your statutes;
and I will keep it to the end.
Give me understanding, that I may keep your law
and observe it with my whole heart.
Lead me in the path of your commandments,
for I delight in it.

— Psalm 119:33-35

Contents

Bible Translations Cited
With Abbreviations and Year Released

KJV — King James Version (1611)

ASV — American Standard Version (1901)

RSV — Revised Standard Version (1952)

NASB — New American Standard Bible (1977, 1995)

NKJV — New King James Version (1982)

NIV — New International Version (1978, 1984, 2011)

NRSV — New Revised Standard Version (1989)

ESV — English Standard Version (2001, 2007, 2011, 2016)

NET — The Net Bible, New English Translation (1996-2016)

Citations from all translations are from the most recently published editions.

Introduction

IN 1983, I WAS hired to teach Bible courses in a Christian school. One of the classes assigned to me that year was the Old Testament survey course we taught to seventh graders.

As I began to plan, I soon realized that I was in a position similar to the veteran football coach who, as the story goes, gathered his team on the first day of practice, held up a ball, and said, "Gentleman, this is a football." He knew that before he could teach his players the finer points and strategies of football, he had to make sure they knew the fundamentals.

Likewise, I knew that before we began the Old Testament survey in Genesis, I needed to teach my students some basics about the Bible. Many of them had attended weekly Bible classes at church since infancy. A significant number had attended our school since kindergarten. But those experiences did not guarantee they knew (or remembered) the basics. Even if all of them did, several of their classmates had different backgrounds and many of that group were newcomers to our school. A Bible course was a new experience for them. I needed to start with the fundamentals.

So, I developed a study unit on basics. What is the Bible? How is it divided? What are its parts? Why do we call its different writings "books"? What are those books? Why study the Bible? What is its story, its plot? Where do the individual books and divisions fit in that story?

Practically speaking, could my students find their way around the Bible? Did they know the names of the books and where each of them is in relation to the others? If asked to look up Ephesians 4:1, did they know what that meant and how to do it? Could they distinguish Ephesians from Ecclesiastes, or 1 Chronicles from 1 Corinthians? Or would they, as more than one student did that year and later, turn to one when I asked them to look up a passage in the other?

Relative to more specific content, did they know the meaning of a term like "old covenant"? Did they know what the Gospels are, or that there are four of them? Did they know the difference between an apostle and an epistle? Experience with different classes over the years proved that questions like these were not hypothetical.

Since no textbook had been assigned to help answer such questions, I wrote short manuscripts on the different topics and distributed them as handouts. Students were assigned to read and answer questions over each one. In class discussions, I went over each handout, fleshing out details, clarifying and elaborating as needed, and making sure they heard the correct answers to the questions. Tests were given after a review of the material.

My decision to teach that unit was validated that year and later by comments and questions of students who showed they did not know the basics. Additional confirmation came from multiple parents, independently over several years, as their sons and daughters joined our student body. Almost word for word, they voiced the same concern. They worried how well their child would do in the class because they "don't really have any background in Bible."

After two or three years, I was assigned to teach other courses to older students. A colleague continued to teach the unit I had written for a few years after that, adding her own creativity to the material. I periodically used parts of it for other courses and the occasional church class. But aside from those exceptions, the material remained in a notebook on a shelf in my library. I would sometimes glance at it as I was looking for a different notebook and think that someday I needed to polish it and make it available in more permanent form. But other demands were always pressing and someday never became today.

Events in early 2018 prompted a different course. A friend told me about a student in a Christian university who had grown up in his congregation and shared with him the observation that other students in his university Bible courses did not seem to know the basic *story* of the Bible. Apparently, they had studied many Bible lessons, but had little sense of how it all fit together.

A few weeks later, another student in the same university shared with me how the church where he had grown up was asking him to teach the teens while he was home for the summer, an assignment they had also given him the previous year. He was concerned that his students did not know the basics. He also lamented that the material he had been given for their class (and would probably be given again) was woefully inadequate to teach what they needed. He asked if I knew of any material that might help.

I recommended a couple of books to him, and also shared with him that I had the material I had prepared thirty-five years before along with a modified version of it that I had used in a church class just a few years ago. I briefly described it and told him I would make copies for him. It was while organizing the material for copying that I thought again that it needed to be reworked. At the time, I was between projects and trying to decide which one to begin next. The timing appeared right for today to finally be someday.

This book is the result. Before you begin, you should know some things I was thinking as I wrote it.

First, I intend it to be a *primer*, an elementary writing that serves as an introduction. It puts into practice an important lesson I've learned about teaching, one I have had reinforced many times. As a teacher, never assume your students know foundational facts or concepts that set the stage for other ideas. At the very least, it's a good idea to ask some questions to find out whether or not they know those things.

Much in this book, especially in its early chapters, will seem obvious to many. But in a world where both formal surveys and experience demonstrate that many people, even among professing Christians, do not know the basics about the Bible, it is evident that these things are not obvious to all. Perhaps one reason many don't know them is because we always assume they do. We need to build (or secure) the foundation.

Second, this book is about the big picture, not the details. In every chapter, more can be said about the subject than I will say. This is especially so in the survey of the entire story in chapter 4 and of its parts in chapters 5-8. I intended only to present an overview. I know the intricacies and nuances of the story are vitally important. But I'm convinced that many of those details often go unappreciated because people do not see the big picture that gives the details their context.

Third, I designed the book to be profitable for individual reading, but also, if desired, to be a resource for Bible class teachers. No, it is not divided into the customary thirteen chapters so common in lesson quarterlies. But the material can be readily adapted for courses of varying duration. It might be a course that lasts only eight weeks. Or, depending on how much a teacher decides to elaborate or how ready students are for more details, it can be used for classes of longer duration. The questions at the end of each chapter, along with the additional notes on individual chapters and the material in the appendices, can facilitate even more explanation and discussion.

Fourth, the chapter questions have multiple purposes. They can be used to review content, the facts in the story. Although many today see facts as tedious, they are the necessary framework for understanding and applying principles. Several questions were written to help teachers determine whether students are understanding the concepts beyond the facts. Others have a component that serve as a catalyst to look deeper, to consider important lessons, meanings, and applications.

Fifth, "there is nothing new under the sun" (Ecclesiastes 1:11). I have learned from the work of many others who have shared their knowledge about the things covered in this book, in both oral and written forms. I have drawn on their work to develop and organize this material. But I have generally adopted a minimalist approach when it comes to citing sources. This decision was made in the interest of leaving the text less cluttered and therefore (I hope) easier to digest.

Sixth, I hope this material will help make the content of the Bible less daunting, a goal that will in turn lead to a greater desire for more study of its story. It is a story with "depth" that is "unsearchable" and "inscrutable." At the same time, it lets us in on many things about "the mind of the Lord," truths we can both understand and be amazed by. It is a "gift" that is increasingly beautiful the more we examine it (quoted words in this paragraph are from Romans 11:33-35).

In Acts 17:1-10, we read about Paul and Silas preaching the story of Jesus in the Macedonian (Greek) town of Thessalonica. Results were mixed. Some were persuaded and joined them. But others persecuted them severely enough that Paul was sent away. People he met in the next town, Berea, shared the same heritage as his Thessalonian persecutors, but their attitude was very different. Acts 17:11 says about them that, "these Jews were more noble than those in Thessalonica; they received the word with all eagerness, examining the Scriptures daily to see if these things were so."

We need more students like the Bereans. I hope you will be one of them and that this brief book will help you as you examine the Scriptures.

Section 1: Basics about the Bible

CHAPTER 1

What Is the Bible?

IMAGINE YOU ARE GOING to put together a jigsaw puzzle. Once assembled, you will have completed a picture of a scene looking across a prairie field of wheat with snowcapped mountains in the background. At the top of the picture will be blue sky with several small white clouds scattered throughout. Oh yes, your puzzle has 500 pieces.

What is the first thing you need to do? I've asked multiple classes to answer that question. Usually, someone will tell me to find the corners and then the edges of the puzzle to build the frame for the picture. When I say that there is something even more basic, someone will usually say that you need to open the box and remove the pieces. But there is something even more basic than that.

The first thing to do before starting to assemble the puzzle pieces is get firmly in mind what the finished puzzle should look like. Where is it most likely that the blue pieces will fit? What about pieces that are green, or those that are brown, or those that are golden? To have an idea of what the completed puzzle should look like and where certain colors are most likely to fit, the first thing to do when starting a puzzle is *look at the picture on the box*! You need to have the big picture in mind to have an idea about how the individual pieces fit.

The same thing is true about Bible study. One must always keep the big picture in mind. Doing that will make the parts of the picture clearer, whether the part you are reading is one of the sixty-six Bible books or a passage within one of those books. Anytime you study anything in the Bible, it is always good to ask where it fits in the big picture.

This book is designed to help you see (or review) the Bible's big picture. We will look at some questions that must be asked about the Bible before trying to do a detailed study of it as a whole or of any of its parts. The specific questions we will address are:

1) What is the Bible?
2) Why should we study the Bible?
3) What is the main story the Bible tells?

This chapter will answer the first question.

Defining the Word "Bible"

Our English word, "Bible" comes from the Greek word *biblos*, which means "book." So, the simplest definition of "Bible" is to say that it is a book.

But the Bible is not just any book. It is more like a library of books. Open your Bible to the list of books (table of contents) at the front. You will immediately notice that the list is long. Upon review, you can see one reason the Bible has sometimes been called "the book of books."

A Different Book

The phrase, "the book of books" is not intended to simply account for the fact that the Bible is made up of a collection of different writings, however. It is a phrase that also calls attention to the fact that the Bible is not an ordinary book. Here are five things about the Bible that distinguish it from other books that we read.

First, the Bible is an older book than most people read. It tells about things that happened thousands of years ago when things were very different from the way they are now. In order to correctly understand how the Bible applies to us today, we must try to understand what it meant then.

Second, the Bible was not originally written in English. Most of the Old Testament was written in Hebrew, with a few sections in the related Aramaic language. The New Testament was written in Greek. English Bibles are translated from those languages. As is always true when translating from one language to another, the words in the ancient biblical languages had specific meanings that do not always have a precise match in the language into which they are being translated. That is why different English translations do not always use the same wording in some passages. It is also why it is a good idea to compare multiple translations when studying a passage. Furthermore, like all languages, Hebrew and Greek had different ways of expressing things, unique idioms that we do not commonly use in modern English. Because of this, we often must use some study tools to do research that helps us have a better understanding of the meaning of Bible passages. While it is helpful to study Hebrew and Greek, one does not have to study those languages to learn a great deal about their world and words. (For examples of the Hebrew and Greek text, see Additional Note 1, p. 21.)

Third, the Bible was written in and about the part of the world we know as the Middle East.[1] The events in the Bible took place around the Mediterranean Sea, and most happened at the eastern end of that body of water. Even today, people in that

---

[1] An important aid to keep handy as one studies the Bible is a source for viewing maps of the regions where the different events occurred. The *ESV Study Bible* (ed. Lane T. Dennis, Wheaton, IL: Crossway Bibles, 2008) includes many excellent maps that are also available online at https://www.esv.org/resources/esv-global-study-bible/article-back-maps/. See also John D. Currid and David P. Barrett, *Crossway ESV Bible Atlas* (Wheaton, IL: Crossway, 2010).

part of the world see things differently than we in the West do. The same kind of differences exist between our cultural setting and the one in which the Bible was written. In order to really understand the Bible, we must seek to understand how the people in that part of the world thought about things.

Fourth, unlike many books we read, the Bible is made up of multiple styles of writing. Some parts of it are stories that are told to illustrate a certain point. Some sections are narratives of events that happened in history. Others are written in poetic style. Still others are written in the form of law codes or drama. And some of the writing is in the form of proverbs, wise observations about life that are generally true.

Many Bible books include just one style of writing (for example, all of the Psalms are poems). But several books include more than one style. For example, Exodus, Leviticus, Numbers, and Deuteronomy contain law codes, historical narratives, and occasional poems. As you study the Bible more, you will learn to identify the different literary styles. You will also want to learn to interpret and understand what is said in each passage according to the kind of writing it is. We read poetry differently than we read historical narratives. Proverbs, allegories, and parables are not read the same way as letters. Law codes are not read the same way as literature written in symbolic language.

Fifth, the story the Bible tells is different. In spite of the fact that the Bible was written by more than 30 people over a time period covering more than 1600 years, it tells one basic story from beginning (Genesis) to end (Revelation). Simply stated, it is the story of God versus evil. More specifically, it is the story of God's plan to help people overcome evil so they can be restored to the right relationship with him that he always intended.

To elaborate on that a little more, from the beginning, God has allowed people the freedom to choose between doing right or wrong. Beginning with Adam and Eve, people have consistently chosen to do wrong. In the language of the Bible, they have chosen to *sin*. Because of sin, people lost the close relationship with God that Adam and Eve once enjoyed and that God wants all people to have. God put into action a plan to allow people to enjoy a relationship with him again. Whether or not we enjoy that relationship depends on whether we trust God and obey his teaching. Since God's plan defeats evil, we can say that the story the Bible tells is a story of great victory!

Why We Need the Bible Now

Perhaps you are wondering, "Why was such an old, different book kept for us in the twenty-first century?" We will notice two important reasons why we need the Bible today.

First, the Bible tells important things about the way people are. It reveals much about the nature of people: our hopes, fears, sorrows, and mistakes. It shows what happens to people when we do the right things. It also shows consequences that result when we do wrong. Finally, it shows that, even though we do wrong, by God's grace and help we can still win a victory over evil.

One way the Bible does this is by honestly presenting the stories of its characters. Think about the Bible's greatest heroes. All of them made mistakes. Some were quite serious. Moses sometimes lost control of his temper. King David committed sexual sin and ordered a murder. Peter got into trouble because he acted and spoke before stopping to think. Paul led others in persecuting and even killing some of God's people. Yet, in each case—and in many others we could mention—God was able to help those people overcome their mistakes and be useful in service to him. From this, we learn that no matter how many mistakes we make, God will help us if we trust him, turn to him, and keep trying to do what he commands.

Second, we need the Bible because of what it tells us about God. The Bible claims that it is not communicating just any message, but the one God has revealed to all people (see for example Exodus 4:10-12; 2 Peter 1:21; and 1 Thessalonians 2:13). The Bible reports things that happened in history, but its aim is not mainly to tell about human history. Instead, it tells about God's nature and how he acted in history to carry out his plan to rescue people so that they can experience a relationship with him.

In light of the Bible's own emphasis on his actions, we can correctly say that God is the principal actor in the story it aims to tell. The main purpose of the Bible is to tell what he is like and what he wants people to be and do.

The Parts of the Bible

The Bible includes sixty-six writings or books. Those books can be organized in different ways. The most basic is the division between the Old and New Testaments.

The first thirty-nine books make up the Old Testament. These writings explain the origin and special mission of the nation of Israel, record the laws God gave to govern the nation, and show how the Israelites lived in relationship with God as his specially chosen people. Sometimes, they did what God commanded, but often they failed. The Old Testament shows that, even when they stumbled, God continued to extend his grace and proceed with his plan to bring people back into a relationship with him.

The last twenty-seven books make up the New Testament. These books tell the story of Jesus' earthly service and are especially concerned to explain the significance of his crucifixion, resurrection, and enthronement as Lord. They also reveal the teachings he gave to guide people who believe in him as the Christ and Son of God, obey him as Lord, and trust him as Savior.

As we will see in chapter 4, the two Testaments go together. They do not tell two separate stories, but are two parts of the one story of God's plan to rescue humanity from the consequences of sin. To put it another way, the Old Testament begins the story that the New Testament completes, and the New Testament finishes the story the Old Testament begins. That story begins with God's promise to Abraham to bless all "the families of the earth" through his offspring (see Genesis 12:1-3). It was completed by Jesus when he carried out his mission to save humanity from sin and commissioned his followers to spread the good news of that salvation "to the ends of the earth" (see Luke 2:32; 24:47; Acts 13:47; 26:23).

The books of both Testaments can be grouped into smaller divisions. The names of the divisions show the kind of writing that is predominant in each of them. We will now look at them more closely.

The Old Testament

As listed in English translations of the Bible, the Old Testament has four divisions, one of which has been sub-divided. (The ancient Israelites organized the books differently. See Additional Note 2, pp. 22-23.)

The first division of the Old Testament includes the books of *Genesis, Exodus, Leviticus, Numbers,* and *Deuteronomy.* They are known as the books of *Law.* The Israelites called them the *Torah,* which essentially means "Instruction." Although the word "Law" is used as the title for this division, we should remember that the law codes recorded in these books are only part of the instruction they include. Much of their content narrates events that explain how Israel came to exist as a nation, the chosen descendants of Abraham through his son Isaac and grandson Jacob (who was renamed Israel; see Genesis 32:27-28). They show how God established a special covenant (agreement) with the people of Israel in commands that he revealed to Moses. Later, the terms of that covenant were used to evaluate whether or not Israel was loyal to God. Throughout their history, when they were obedient, they loyally followed the commands written in these five books.

The second division of the Old Testament includes the books of *Joshua, Judges, Ruth, 1 & 2 Samuel, 1 & 2 Kings, 1 & 2*

Chronicles, Ezra, Nehemiah, and *Esther.* It is called the *History* division. These books tell how Israel conquered and lived in Canaan, the land where God had promised Abraham his descendants would live (see Genesis 12:7; 17:8). When they kept their agreement with God and obeyed his commands, they were blessed. But they were not always obedient, and so these books also show examples of times when the people were not faithful to the agreement with God that is spelled out in the *Torah.* When they failed, God held them accountable and judged them. Because of their disloyalty, the land God promised to give them was conquered by foreign rulers and many of the Israelites were exiled to the homelands of those empires. In all, these books cover events that occurred over about 1,000 years of Israelite history.

The third division of the Old Testament includes the books of *Job, Psalms, Proverbs, Ecclesiastes,* and *Song of Solomon.* These are the books of *Poetry.* They show the range of emotions God's people experienced as they faced the ups and down of life. They especially reveal how the people sometimes asked hard questions about the trials they faced. The different books—and even parts of some of them—come from various times in the historical periods covered in the books of Law and History.

The books in the fourth Old Testament division are the *Prophets.* These seventeen books record the efforts of faithful servants who were called by God to try to convince unfaithful Israelites to remain loyal to their covenant with him. The books often show why the nation was experiencing trouble and declare the consequences Israel faced because of the people's disobedience. But they also include statements of hope about God's future plans of deliverance and restoration. The prophets lived at different times in the later years of the time period covered in the History division.

The Prophets are divided into two sections. The first five, known as the *Major Prophets,* are *Isaiah, Jeremiah, Lamen-*

tations, Ezekiel, and *Daniel.* The word "major" is not used to mean that these five books are more important than the other twelve, but because they are generally longer than the other books and are listed separately in the Hebrew classification of the writings.

The last twelve books are the *Minor Prophets,* a group that includes *Hosea, Joel, Amos, Obadiah, Jonah, Micah, Nahum, Habakkuk, Zephaniah, Haggai, Zechariah,* and *Malachi.* Again, the word "minor" does not mean these books are considered less important. Instead, it indicates that they are generally shorter than the first five. In the Hebrew organization of the books, they were collected as one book, called "The Twelve."

The New Testament

The New Testament also has four divisions. The first includes *Matthew, Mark, Luke,* and *John,* the books known as the *Gospels.* The English word "gospel" translates a Greek word (*euaggelion*) that meant "good news." It is therefore a good title for this division that is devoted to telling the story of Jesus, the Son of God and humanity's Savior.

It is important to know what these books do and how they do it. The Gospels are sometimes called "biographies," and they are like other *ancient* biographies that have survived from the same culture and time period. But they were not written like *modern* biographies. They report things about Jesus' life that really did happen, but they do not try to cover his entire life in sequence from birth to death. In fact, some parts of his life receive no attention at all. John's statement about what he aimed to do in his Gospel shows the approach taken by all four of the writers. He wrote:

> Now Jesus did many other signs in the presence of the disciples, which are not written in this book; but these are written so that you may believe that Jesus is the Christ, the Son of God, and that by believing you may have life in his name (John 20:30-31).

17

We should notice three things in this passage. First, John said that he had been selective in what he included. In other words, he did not try to tell everything Jesus did, just some of the things he did (see John 21:25). Second, he did not say that he was reporting the things he included in chronological order. This does not mean that he told things that did not really happen, but that he selected things from what did happen and organized them for a particular purpose. Third, he revealed what that purpose was. He said that he wrote what he did in order to help his readers come to believe that "Jesus is the Christ, the Son of God."

We can compare the Gospels to modern documentaries that present information about a person in a topical order instead of chronologically. For example, if I wanted to produce a documentary that showed what a great basketball player Michael Jordan was, I would include sections that focus specifically on his ability as a shooter, passer, and defender. I would no doubt add a section devoted to some of his spectacular dunks. In each case, I would select examples of the skill being showcased in that segment. The examples chosen would not necessarily be in chronological order. And my documentary would probably not say much at all about his life apart from basketball. My purpose would be only to present him as a basketball player. But in telling that story, everything that I would choose to include would have really happened.

In the same way, as John 20:30-31 indicates, the Gospel writers selected things that happened in the life of Jesus for the purpose of *convincing* people that "Jesus is the Christ, the Son of God" (John 20:31) and therefore the Savior of humanity. That is why they devoted more space to the details of his death by crucifixion and his resurrection from the dead. It is significant that, in all four Gospels, proportionately more is said about his death and resurrection than about the other events of his life.

The second division of the New Testament includes only the book of *Acts*, a book of *History*. It tells how his disciples continued Jesus' mission, beginning in Jerusalem, where he had died and was raised, and where the church began. They convinced others that he was Lord and Christ (see Acts 2:36) and the church began to increase and spread throughout the world (compare Acts 2:41; 4:4; 6:7; 12:24; 19:20). Acts tells about followers of Jesus who went out from Jerusalem to the surrounding regions of Judea and Samaria, and then continued across the Roman Empire. It ends with Paul's arrival and preaching in Rome, the empire's capital city. The book covers about the first thirty years of the church's existence, and focuses on how the story of Jesus spread west from Jerusalem, north of the Mediterranean Sea, and then to Rome. The two people primarily featured in the book are Peter and Paul. A good way to remember the purpose of Acts is to note that it shows how a person *converts* to Jesus.

The third New Testament division is made up of twenty-one *Epistles*. These books are letters to selected believers and churches throughout the Roman Empire. They were written to strengthen, teach, and encourage them as they faced different problems in practicing their faith. Part of the teaching and encouragement took the form of correcting misunderstandings and behaviors that were not as they should have been. Since the aim of these books is to help Christians become stronger, we can say that the purpose of the epistles is to *confirm* Christian believers in their faith.

Like the Old Testament Prophets, the Epistles have been divided into two sections. The first thirteen are the *Pauline Epistles*, the writings of the apostle Paul. They were written to specific churches or individuals. These books are *Romans, 1 & 2 Corinthians, Galatians, Ephesians, Philippians, Colossians, 1 & 2 Thessalonians, 1 & 2 Timothy, Titus,* and *Philemon*.

The remaining eight are called *General Epistles* because they were written to more general audiences, sometimes to a group of churches in a geographical area. They are less personal than Paul's letters, more like official letters or sermons sent from church leaders to a group of churches. These books are *Hebrews, James, 1 & 2 Peter, 1, 2, & 3 John*, and *Jude*.

The last section of the New Testament is the division of *Prophecy*. Like the History division, it includes just one writing, the book of *Revelation*. It is written in figurative and symbolic language (in a style known as apocalyptic writing; see note [10] on p. 106). Students of the book have long debated the specific meaning of many of the details in the figures used in Revelation. The book's main point is clear, however. It was written at a time when God's people were facing trials in the form of active opposition. It aims to reassure them that, no matter how bad things may be or seem, God has and always will overcome evil. It assures God's people that all who trust in him will be victorious. Revelation is designed to *console* God's people when they face trouble.

Conclusion

The Bible is a unique book. It is ancient, yet always relevant to the lives of modern people. It matters because it deals with concerns and problems that people still face. The Bible reveals what God has done to help people find the life that is ultimately satisfying and eternal (compare John 10:10; 17:3). It is a book that deserves our attention and study.

Additional Note 1: Examples of Hebrew and Greek Text

Unlike English and other Western languages, Hebrew is written from right to left, and the Bible books are printed in order from what would be the back of an English book to the front.

Here is Genesis 1:1 as it appears in a modern edition of the Hebrew Bible, followed by the ESV's translation of the verse.

בְּרֵאשִׁית בָּרָא אֱלֹהִים אֵת הַשָּׁמַיִם וְאֵת הָאָרֶץ׃

In the beginning, God created the heavens and the earth.

Like English, Greek is written from left to right and books are arranged from what we view as front to back in a book. Here is John 3:16 as printed in a modern edition of the Greek New Testament, followed by the ESV's translation of the verse.

οὕτως γὰρ ἠγάπησεν ὁ θεὸς τὸν κόσμον, ὥστε τὸν υἱὸν τὸν μονογενῆ ἔδωκεν, ἵνα πᾶς ὁ πιστεύων εἰς αὐτὸν μὴ ἀπόληται ἀλλ᾽ ἔχῃ ζωὴν αἰώνιον.

For God so loved the world, that he gave his only Son, that whoever believes in him should not perish but have eternal life.

Additional Note 2: Hebrew Arrangement and Classification of the Old Testament

The Jewish arrangement of the books Christians know as the Old Testament divides them into three sections, "Law, Prophets, and Writings." Sometimes, the designation was shortened to "the Law and the Prophets" (compare Matthew 7:12; Luke 16:16; etc.). (Note: In Luke 24:44, Jesus referred to the Scriptures as the "Law, Prophets, and Psalms." Some think this is an alternate way of referring to the three-part division mentioned above, chosen because Psalms was the book that appeared at the beginning of the third section, the Writings.)

In this arrangement, the Prophets section is divided into "Former Prophets" and "Latter Prophets." The "Former Prophets" include six books that are found in the History Division in the English classification. The "Latter Prophets" include the seventeen writing prophets collected as the Prophets in the English classification.

A few of the books that are listed separately in the English classification are combined as single books in the Jewish arrangement. These include the books known to us as the "Minor Prophets," which were collected as "the Twelve." Because of these combinations, there are twenty-four books in the Jewish list. The content of the books is the same as the thirty-nine books in the English list.

Both arrangements are included in the following chart.

Old Testament, English	Jewish Classification	New Testament
Law (5)	**Torah (5)**	**Gospels (4)**
Genesis	Genesis	Matthew
Exodus	Exodus	Mark
Leviticus	Leviticus	Luke
Numbers	Numbers	John
Deuteronomy	Deuteronomy	**History (1)**
History (12)	**Former Prophets (4)**	Acts
Joshua	Joshua	**Paul's Epistles (13)**
Judges	Judges	Romans
Ruth	1-2 Samuel (one book)	1 Corinthians
1 Samuel	1-2 Kings (one book)	2 Corinthians
2 Samuel	**Latter Prophets (4)**	Galatians
1 Kings	Isaiah	Ephesians
2 Kings	Jeremiah	Philippians
1 Chronicles	Ezekiel	Colossians
2 Chronicles	The Twelve (one book)	1 Thessalonians
Ezra	*Hosea* *Nahum*	
Nehemiah	*Joel* *Habakkuk*	2 Thessalonians
Esther	*Amos* *Zephaniah*	1 Timothy
Poetry (5)	*Obadiah* *Haggai*	2 Timothy
Job	*Jonah* *Zechariah*	Titus
Psalms	*Micah* *Malachi*	Philemon
Proverbs	**The Writings (11)**	**General Epistles (8)**
Ecclesiastes	Psalms	Hebrews
Song of Solomon	Job	James
Major Prophets (5)	Proverbs	1 Peter
Isaiah	Ruth	2 Peter
Jeremiah	Song of Solomon	1 John
Lamentations	Ecclesiastes	2 John
Ezekiel	Lamentations	3 John
Daniel	Esther	Jude
Minor Prophets (12)	Daniel	**Prophecy (1)**
Hosea Nahum	Ezra-Nehemiah (one book)	Revelation
Joel Habakkuk	1-2 Chronicles (one book)	
Amos Zephaniah		
Obadiah Haggai		
Jonah Zechariah		
Micah Malachi		

For Review and Thought

1. Explain what assembling a jigsaw puzzle illustrates about studying the Bible.

2. What three things must be understood before we can understand any part of the Bible?

3. Give the most basic definition of the word "Bible" and explain why it has sometimes been called "the book of books."

4. List five things we need to understand about the Bible in order to know what kind of book the Bible is.

5. In what languages was the Old Testament originally written? The New Testament?

6. In what part of the world do the events described in the Bible take place?

7. What story does the Bible tell?

8. Why was the Bible kept for modern people?

9. Who is the principal actor in the Bible's story? What is its main purpose?

10. List three Bible passages that illustrate the claim that the message in the Bible comes from God.

11. Take some time to learn the books of the Bible (in order), the main divisions of the Bible, the number of books in each division, the major divisions in each Testament, and the specific books in each division.

CHAPTER 2

Why Study the Bible?

NOW THAT WE KNOW more about the Bible's makeup, we are ready to consider why we should study it. Why invest so much time and energy to learn the contents of such an old book that comes from a different part of the world and tells about the lives of people who died thousands of years ago?

The short answer? The Bible is God's revelation to humanity. More specifically, in the Bible, God has provided instruction that tells us how to live the way we were created to live. He has revealed the knowledge we need to realize our true purpose.

We can illustrate this by thinking about some of the devices we have that help make our lives easier. For example, it is possible to learn to drive a car without knowing anything more than how to start it, put it in gear, and travel to the destination we choose. But newer cars have accessories that make our experience of traveling easier than it was for our parents and grandparents. The more we know about how to use these accessories, the more we benefit from having them in the car. The same can be said about other devices such as smart phones, microwave ovens, the machines that wash and dry our clothes, or the computer I am using to write this book.

God created people in his image and has revealed how we should live in order to receive the most joy and benefit from life. The Bible reveals his instruction in words that we can understand. We will benefit more from studying it if we know its specific purposes.

A New Testament passage written by Paul is especially helpful for beginning to understand these purposes. This passage is from a letter Paul wrote to some Christians in the ancient city of Colossae, a town located in what is now the nation of Turkey. He wrote:

> 9 And so, from the day we heard, we have not ceased to pray for you, asking that you may be filled with the knowledge of his will in all spiritual wisdom and understanding, 10 so as to walk in a manner worthy of the Lord, fully pleasing to him: bearing fruit in every good work and increasing in the knowledge of God; 11 being strengthened with all power, according to his glorious might, for all endurance and patience with joy; 12 giving thanks to the Father, who has qualified you to share in the inheritance of the saints in light. 13 He has delivered us from the domain of darkness and transferred us to the kingdom of his beloved Son, 14 in whom we have redemption, the forgiveness of sins (Colossians 1:9-14).

In these verses, Paul told the Colossians about his ongoing prayer for them. In effect, his petitions expand on the brief rationale for Bible study we noted above, pointing to three specific reasons to study it. His prayer also refers to some benefits of Bible study. We will therefore look more closely at Paul's prayer, beginning with the reasons for study it reveals.

Learning What God Thinks

The first thing he asked for in his prayer was for the Colossians to "be filled with the knowledge of [God's] will." To say it another way, *the first reason to study the Bible is because it is in the Bible that we learn what God thinks about life's great questions.* It is also where he teaches what he intends for all people to be and do. Learning what God thinks and intends is what it means to "know the will of God."

As we think about the process involved, we must always remember that we are not like God. His thoughts are not like our thoughts. His ways are not like our ways. To compare ourselves with him is like comparing the distance between the height of the heavens and the lowliness of the earth (Isaiah 55:8-9). We must also remember that God is a living being whose nature is spirit (John 4:24). His understanding and power are infinitely greater than the knowledge and strength we have (see Psalm 147:5; Isaiah 46:10).

Since God is so different from us, how is it possible to know what he is thinking? Furthermore, since he is far superior to us in every way, how can he possibly communicate what he thinks to us in ways we can comprehend? In another letter he wrote to the church in Corinth (in Greece), Paul answered both of those questions.

> 6 Yet among the mature we do impart wisdom, although it is not a wisdom of this age or of the rulers of this age, who are doomed to pass away. 7 But we impart a secret and hidden wisdom of God, which God decreed before the ages for our glory. 8 None of the rulers of this age understood this, for if they had, they would not have crucified the Lord of glory. 9 But, as it is written,
> "What no eye has seen, nor ear heard,
>   nor the heart of man imagined,
>   what God has prepared for those who love him" —
> 10 these things God has revealed to us through the Spirit. For the Spirit searches everything, even the depths of God. 11 For who knows a person's thoughts except the spirit of that person, which is in him? So also no one comprehends the thoughts of God except the Spirit of God. 12 Now we have received not the spirit of the world, but the Spirit who is from God, that we might understand the things freely given us by God. 13 And we impart this in words not taught by human wisdom but taught by the Spirit, interpreting spiritual truths to those who are spiritual (1 Corinthians 2:6-13; v. 9 is a quotation from Isaiah 64:4).

Verses 6-9 continue the thought Paul began in 1 Corinthians 1:18: from a human viewpoint, the message of the gospel is not what the thinkers of this age consider to be wisdom. Indeed, Paul said, "the foolishness of God is wiser than men, . . ." (1:25). Furthermore, "God chose what is foolish in the world to shame the wise" (1:27). That does not mean the message of the gospel is not wise, however. The gospel is the revelation of God's wisdom that far surpasses "the wisdom of this age" (2:8).

How can anyone ever know God's matchless wisdom, his thoughts? We can know what God thinks the same way we can know the thoughts of anyone. In 1 Corinthians 2:10-13, Paul said that the only way we can ever know what someone else is thinking in his spirit is if that person decides to reveal it to us. In the same way, God's thoughts were known by his Spirit who revealed them to selected people in understandable words. Those people shared those words with others, in both spoken and written form. Any person who hears or reads the revealed words can know and understand what God thinks.

How important is it to know and understand what God is thinking? Let's follow Paul's example and compare the process to the way we know what another human being is thinking. We'll use the world's heads of state to illustrate. Whether the official's title is King, Premier, President, Prime Minister, or some other, it is important for citizens of the ruler's nation to know what he or she is thinking. In fact, it matters for how they live. Suppose a king is thinking about leading his nation into war, a conflict that might last several years. For a younger person who could be called to serve in the armed forces, the king's thinking about going to war will make a big difference. In a different way, it will also matter to the parents or grandparents of someone who might be called on to fight. And if the war is to be fought within the borders of the king's country, what he thinks about going to war will matter even more to everyone.

How can citizens find out what their leader is thinking? In theory at least, it is possible they could be invited to his or her office or residence for a meeting where they would be told directly. It is far more likely that they will learn it from a speech, official statement, or news report. But however they learn them, rulers must choose to reveal their thoughts before anyone can know them.

Now, if knowing what a powerful person such as a king or president thinks is important to us, how much more important is it to know what God thinks? No matter how knowledgeable our heads of state are, they are not as knowledgeable as God. No matter how powerful they are, God's power is greater. Surely, then, we can see that if God wants us to live in a way that is best for us, it is important for us to know what he thinks.

How can we know what God is thinking? As we saw above in 1 Corinthians 2:10-13, we can know because he has revealed it and seen to it that what he revealed has been written in words that we can read and understand (see Ephesians 3:3-5). When we read the Bible, we learn what God thinks and intends. The process is the same as the one we use to find out what a king or president thinks and intends. The difference is that we learn the ruler's thoughts from newspapers, radio, video, or social media while God's thoughts and intentions are communicated in the pages of the Bible. But we will not learn what it says unless we read and study it.

More Than the Facts

The second reason we should study the Bible is because it helps us gain wisdom and insight into the ways of God. In Colossians 1:9, Paul said that God does not want us to just read or hear the words he has revealed to us. He wants us to understand what he says and act wisely because we know his words. In Paul's words, God wants us to have "spiritual wisdom and understanding" about his will.

29

It is important to know that, in the Greek text, the language in which the New Testament was first written, the grammatical structure in verse 9 indicates that the adjective "spiritual" modifies both "wisdom" and "understanding." In other words, we are to understand the words God revealed in his will with wisdom that is spiritually inclined and with understanding, or insight, that is also spiritually inclined. A good way to see the significance of this point is to break down the parts of the process involved in learning, understanding, and acting on the will of God. Stated in brief form, we should:

- Know what the Bible says about God and what we should do to please him.
- Understand what the Bible says and what those teachings mean.
- Act on what the Bible says in the way we live our lives.

To do these things, we must study the Bible for within its pages we will read what we need to know to chart our course in this life and have eternal life (see Proverbs 14:12; Jeremiah 10:23; John 10:10; 17:3; 2 Timothy 3:15). But we gain this knowledge only by studying and growing in our understanding of God's word and the spiritual wisdom he wants us to have (compare 1 Peter 2:2; 2 Peter 3:18). Once we have learned what God said and developed understanding of what it means, it is up to us to live the way God wants us to live.

What the Bible Should Do In Our Lives

The third reason to study the Bible is because it will positively change our lives. Colossians 1:10 points to three things it does for us.

To Please God

First, Paul said that knowing and understanding the will of God should lead us "to walk in a manner worthy of the Lord, fully pleasing to him." Paul was a Jew who had been well taught the beliefs and ways of expressing them commonly used by his people. The Jews used the word "walk" as a figure of speech to refer to the way people live their lives. That is why the New International Version (NIV) translates the first part of verse 10 this way: "so that you may *live a life worthy of the Lord* and please him in every way." Together, God's nature and laws establish a high standard for behavior. People who are "fully pleasing to him" will do their best to live in a way that comes as close as possible to that standard. This is what it means to "live a life worthy of the Lord."

God does not want people to simply learn what the Bible says and be able to repeat back that information. Certainly, it is important to learn what it says well enough to talk about it in an informed way, but unless we act on what we learn, we will not realize the true goal of Bible study. The teachings of the Bible should be learned so well that they begin to become part of who we are and define how we live. The goal is not just to learn the words, but to internalize them so that we come to naturally please God in the way we think and live.

Bearing Fruit in Every Good Work

Second, Paul said that the Bible's content equips us to "bear fruit in every good work." "Bearing fruit" is another figure of speech used to describe how people should live. This figure points to two ideas.

First, it indicates that people who are pleasing God should be productive. Just as an apple tree that does what it is supposed to do will produce apples (or a peach tree will produce peaches, and so on), so people will show whether they have learned the will of God by the kind of behavior they produce.

Second, the idea of bearing fruit means that the fruit that is produced should be like the kind of tree on which it grows. Good apple trees will not produce peaches or pears. If they are good trees, they will also not produce rotten apples. In the same way, people who are bearing fruit that is worthy of God will produce good fruit that looks like God's holy character (compare Exodus 19:6; Leviticus 11:45; Hebrews 12:10; 1 Peter 1:14-16).

To determine the kind of fruit we are to produce, we need to study the Bible where we will find passages that specify what the fruit of a person pleasing God will be like. One of the most important passages in this regard is found in Galatians 5. In verses 19-21, Paul describes behaviors, which he calls "the works of the flesh," that are ugly and unproductive. He specifically mentions "sexual immorality, impurity, sensuality, idolatry, sorcery, enmity, strife, jealousy, fits of anger, rivalries, dissensions, divisions, envy, drunkenness, orgies, and things like these." People who persist in doing these things "will not inherit the kingdom of God."

In verses 22 and 23, he lists attitudes and character traits that are beautiful and productive, the opposite of "the works of the flesh." Collectively, Paul called these behaviors "the fruit [singular, not 'fruits'] of the Spirit." He wrote, "But the fruit of the Spirit is love, joy, peace, patience, kindness, goodness, faithfulness, gentleness, self-control; against such things there is no law."

Think about how wonderful it would be to live in a society where everyone showed love, was determined to be at peace, and always practiced patience, kindness, goodness, faithfulness, gentleness, and self-control. Surely, a society like that would be a better place to live than one in which people pursue lives committed to the works of the flesh listed in verses 19-21. A life characterized by the traits of "the fruit of the Spirit" is what pleases God. Studying the Bible, and especially the character and behavior of Jesus, will help us be the kind of people who live in the way that is worthy of the Lord.

Increasing in the Knowledge of God

Third, Paul said that knowing God's revelation is important because it gives us what we need to "increase in the knowledge of God." At first glance, we may think that this phrase simply repeats Paul's first request, that believers will be "filled with the knowledge of his will." In fact, the two phrases express different ideas and "increasing in the knowledge of God" is the ultimate goal of Bible study.

What does it mean to "increase in the knowledge of God"? To help answer that question, think about one of the celebrities who are often in the news. Maybe it's a singer, an actor, a government leader, or an athlete. For purposes of this exercise, it can't be someone you have ever met.

Since I'm a baseball fan, I'll choose a former major league player who starred on the team I rooted for as a child. He played centerfield in the first major league baseball game I attended many years ago. I can tell you what kind of player he was. I can tell you how many hits he got in his career, and how many were doubles, triples, and home runs. I can tell you where he was born, his race, and where he died. I can tell you some of the challenges he faced, not just as a baseball player, but as a victim of the immoral discrimination that was more blatant in the era when he played. Because I happened to discover and follow a Facebook page maintained by his son, I can tell you the name of that son and pass along some of his recollections about his father. I can also tell you that the view that he was an outstanding player is not just the product of idealized memories from my childhood. I can refer you to sports writers, people who played with or against him, and others who will testify to just how good a player he was, not to mention that he was also a kind and considerate man.

But here's the thing: I never met him, or even got close enough to him at a game or anywhere else to talk with him or get his autograph. My knowledge of him is secondhand, and is limited to things I know *about* him, not knowledge *of* him. I never had a personal relationship with him.

That is the difference in Colossians 1:9-10 between knowing the will of God and having knowledge of God. We can learn many things about God and what he thinks without ever developing a personal relationship with him. Please do not misunderstand what I am saying. It is necessary to know some things about a person in order to have knowledge of that person. So, the better we know God's attributes and details of his will, the better foundation we have for knowing him. But the two kinds of knowing are not the same.

The Bible emphasizes many times how much God wants us to know him, not just know about him. Among the Old Testament examples of this truth are passages in Hosea (who prophesied about 745-715 BC) and Jeremiah (who prophesied about 626-565 BC). Both prophets rebuked the Israelite people for thinking that just because they had and knew about the Law, the temple, and other things that God had revealed to them, they did not need to know him and treat their relationship with obedient respect (see Jeremiah 2:8; 31:34; Hosea 2:20; 4:1, 6; 5:4; 6:3, 6; 8:2; 13:4).

In the New Testament, Paul said that some who were immoral in their behavior acted that way because they did not know God (1 Thessalonians 4:5). He said that his goal above everything else was to know Christ Jesus (Philippians 3:8). In other letters, Peter and John also stressed the importance of knowing God (see 2 Peter 1:2; 2:20; 3:18; 1 John 2:3-5, 14; 4:2, 6-8; 5:20).

The most signifiant statement of the idea, however, comes from Jesus himself. In John 17:3, he defined "eternal life" as knowing the only true God and Jesus Christ whom he sent. Since Jesus defined eternal life as knowing God, it is necessary for us to seek that knowledge. Bible study is one of the things we must do to bring that about.

At this point it is important to stress that what we are talking about is a process in which we must remain engaged throughout our lives. Once again, an illustration will help us see the point. Think about someone you have met and know personally. It may be a close friend, a dear family member, or a spouse. Before you developed a relationship with that person, you no doubt learned some things about him or her. But you

have almost certainly found
that getting to know them better has created opportunities
for learning even more about
them.

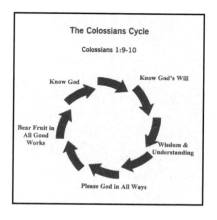

The same will be true
in our relationship with God.
The greater our knowledge *of*
him is, the more we will find
that we are learning *about* him.
The process described in
Colossians 1:9-10 becomes repetitive. Our greater knowledge
about him and his will leads to more spiritual wisdom and understanding. We learn more about what pleases him and how
to walk more faithfully in a way that is worthy of him. That in
turn leads to even greater knowledge of him. The cycle will be
repeated, over and over as long as we live. (The figure, "The
Colossians Cycle," illustrates this process and its ongoing nature.)

Benefits of Bible Study

Before we conclude this chapter, we should notice one other
aspect of Paul's prayer for the Colossians. Verses 11-14 identify
five benefits that result from the process we have examined
from verses 9-10.

Verse 11 says that coming to know God allows believers
to be *"strengthened with all power,* according to his glorious
might, for all endurance and patience with joy." Life is often
not easy. We face difficulties associated with being finite beings in a world where calamities can strike, illnesses can afflict
us, we lose our strength, and must face death. Sin and its consequences bring additional trouble. We need strength to en-
dure and wisdom to develop the patience that helps us face
trouble with joy (see James 1:2-4). Knowing God's will, gaining
spiritual wisdom and understanding, living in a manner that is

worthy of the Lord, and then increasing in our knowledge of God strengthens us to face these trials.

Verse 12 adds that those who know God have been "qualified" by him "to share in the inheritance of the saints of light." "Saints" is translated from the Greek word for holiness (the NIV translates the word, "holy people"). No matter who we are, or what we have done, continuing in the process that leads us to increase in our knowledge of God means that we can be confident that we will share the blessings of inheritance that will be given to all people who imitate and share God's holiness (see 1 Peter 1:15; Hebrews 12:10).

Verse 13 says that when we come to know God, we also know that he has "delivered us from the domain of darkness and transferred us to the kingdom of his beloved Son." The Greek verb translated "delivered" (*hruomai*) was used in the third century BC Greek translation of the Old Testament to refer to God's deliverance of the Israelites from their slavery to the Egyptians. Exodus 14:30 explains Israel's escape from their Egyptian pursuers by passing through the Red Sea on dry ground, saying, "Thus the LORD *saved* Israel that day from the hand of the Egyptians, and Israel saw the Egyptians dead on the seashore" (see also Exodus 12:27 which refers to how the Lord "spared" the houses of Israel during the tenth plague). For the word translated "saved" in verse 30 (and "spared" in 12:27), the Greek translators used the same word translated "delivered" in Colossians 1:13 (*hruomai*). Paul's use of that word recalls the memory of Israel's deliverance and applies it to the spiritual deliverance from the power of sin that Christ's followers receive, what Paul called "the domain of darkness."

Verse 14 mentions two other benefits of knowing God. First, Paul said that those who know God have "redemption." This word was used to refer to releasing or being set free and was often used to refer to liberation of slaves. It was also used to describe the deliverance of the Israelites from Egypt and then to refer to the deliverance of the people from the control of the Babylonians after their exile (see Deuteronomy 7:8; 9:26; 13:6; 15:5; Psalms 74:2; 77:16; Isaiah 41:14; 43:1, 14; 44:22-24; 52:3; 54:5).

Second, Paul said that those who know God have "forgiveness of sins." The word translated "forgiveness" was used to refer to having a debt cancelled. It is used in verse 14 to further explain the meaning of "redemption." Believers are freed from sin when the debt caused by their failure is cancelled (see Romans 6:7).

Conclusion

The goals Paul prayed the Colossians would reach and the benefits they would receive as they pursued them are available to all who know, understand, and build lives on the things God revealed in his word. That means that Bible study is one of the most important things we can ever do. It will make a difference in how we live and enjoy the lives God has given to us. It will also help us prepare for the everlasting life to come. God knows what is best for each of us and has communicated it for us to learn. He did so because he wants us to know him. We are wise therefore to make Bible study a regular part of our lives.

For Review and Thought

1. Identify the reasons for studying the Bible discussed in this chapter. Set a goal to memorize Colossians 1:9-10.

2. What is the significance of Isaiah 55:8-9 for Bible study?

3. What is the only way we can ever know what someone else is thinking? Explain what 1 Corinthians 2:6-13 shows about learning what God is thinking. Why is it important to know what God thinks?

4. Who did Paul say was the only one who "comprehends the things of God"?

5. What method did Paul say God's Spirit used to communicate God's thoughts to us? What is necessary on our part if we are to learn what he has said?

6. Explain what is meant by "spiritual wisdom and understanding" and the three-step process we identified for coming to have this wisdom and understanding.

7. Identify the three things Colossians 1:10 says the Bible does to change our lives in a positive way.

8. Explain the meaning of the word "walk" in Colossians 1:10 and what a person should do to be "fully pleasing" to God.

9. What two things are indicated by the figure of "bearing fruit"? What will be produced by a person who is bearing fruit that is worthy of God?

10. What are the traits that together make up "the fruit of the Spirit" (Galatians 5:22-23)?

11. Explain the difference between knowing about someone and having knowledge of that person. Identify some important passages from the Old and New Testaments that emphasize the importance of knowing God.

12. How did Jesus define "eternal life" and why is that significant?

13. Explain and identify the parts of what we called "The Colossians Cycle."

14. Name the five benefits of Bible study found in Colossians 1:11-14.

15. Based on this chapter, explain how you would answer if someone asked you why they should study the Bible.

CHAPTER 3

Using Book, Chapter, and Verse Abbreviations

BIBLE STUDY HAS BEEN made easier for us by the division of the books into chapters and verses. Like other writings of the time, the books of the Bible were originally written on scrolls that had to be unrolled to find a specific passage. We see an example of what that meant in practice in the Gospel of Mark. Some members of a Jewish party known as the Sadducees asked Jesus a question which they thought showed the impossibility of resurrection. In response, he said, "And as for the dead being raised, have you not read *in the book of Moses, in the passage about the bush,* how God spoke to him, saying, 'I am the God of Abraham, and the God of Isaac, and the God of Jacob'?" (Mark 12:26). To read the passage Jesus referred to, a person in his time would have been required to unroll the correct scroll and find the reference to "the passage about the bush."

Today, we open a Bible and turn to Exodus 3:1-4 to find the account of Moses and the burning bush. The shorthand references we just used (Mark 12:26; Exodus 3:1-4) are examples of another development that makes Bible study easier. We use standard abbreviations and notations to refer to the Bible passages. Without this shorthand, we would have been required to write out the passages cited above. That would look something like this: In Mark, chapter 12, verse twenty-six, Jesus reminded his critics of the teaching of the passage found in Exodus chapter three, verses one through four.

Newcomers to Bible study may not immediately recognize what the abbreviations and notations for Bible references mean. Because they are commonly used in the books we read about the Bible, most of us figure them out over time. This chapter seeks to shorten the process by reviewing some "rules" that are used in this shorthand.

Before we begin, I should make you aware of two things. First, I am using the word "rules" in this chapter only as a way to designate the particular guidelines I am talking about. They are not rules in the sense a football game has rules, or in the sense the phrase "obeying the rules" is used as a synonym for doing what a nation's laws require. In fact, depending on the writer or publisher, you will find variations in the way the Bible books are abbreviated and even in specific styles used to cite references. What follows are the most commonly used abbreviations and citations.

Second, I wrote these guidelines based on my experiences as a learning Bible student. Others may have written similar material, but I do not recall ever reading a comparable discussion. Again, I present them merely to spell out how they are typically done in order to accelerate the learning process for beginning Bible students who may be unfamiliar with the rules.

Six Basic Rules

Rule 1: Use a colon (:) to distinguish between a chapter and a verse. For example, Matthew, chapter 22, verse 5, is written "Matthew 22:5." "Isaiah 7:21" refers to the twenty-first verse of Isaiah's seventh chapter. Acts 13, verse 5 is written "Acts 13:5," and so on. [Note: some authors use a period instead of a colon; when that is done, the examples we just used are written this way: Matthew 22.5; Isaiah 7.21; Acts 13.5.]

Rule 2: Use a semi-colon (;) between citations when several passages are listed in a series. The semi-colon is used for two different kinds of citations.

First, a writer may want to list several references from different books. For example, he might write, "The teaching of the New Testament is that Jesus existed as God throughout eternity and was involved in creating the world before being sent to the earth to live as a man (John 1:1-14; Hebrews 1:1-3; Philippians 2:5-8)." Notice the colon in each reference to separate the chapter and verse references (rule 1). But notice also the semi-colons that are used to separate the references to the passages in the different books from each other (rule 2). The semi-colons make it easier for us to see that different passages are being cited and to distinguish between them.

A second use of the semi-colon to separate references helps distinguish between different chapters from the same book. For example, a writer who wants to call attention to some of the passages in the book of Acts that show what people did when they converted to Jesus would list the references this way: Acts 2:38-41; 8:12; 16:31. The colons tell us which chapters and verses in the book are being cited (rule 1). The semi-colons separate the different chapters from which the citations come (rule 2).

Rule 3: Commas (,) are used to separate items of equal importance in a series. As with semi-colons, commas are used to separate items in two different kinds of series.

First, a writer will use commas to show that he is referring to different chapters within a book. He might write, "One of the important subjects in Paul's letter to the Romans is the idea that to live by faith means that one will live the kind of life that shows he or she is committed to obeying God (Romans 6, 8, 12, 13)." The commas, without the use of colons or semi-colons, show that we need to study the chapters that are listed in order to confirm the point the writer makes about Paul's teaching about faith and obedience.

A second use of commas separates a series of verses within one chapter of a book. A writer might say, "In his sermon on the day of Pentecost, Peter told his hearers that Jesus had been raised from the dead and that his resurrection showed that he was the Christ the Jews had been waiting for God to send (Acts 2:24, 29, 32, 33)." The colon shows that the author is citing the second chapter of Acts (rule 1). The use of commas instead of semi-colons shows that all the verses cited are from the same chapter. The commas also show that the writer intends to refer to only the specific verses listed to show the point he is making (rule 3).

Rule 4: Use a hyphen (-) to connect items in a wider range of passages in which everything within the range is to be studied. Once again, the rule is used in more than one way.

First, a writer may intend to refer to something that is discussed in every chapter in a group where all are located together. Instead of listing all of them and using commas to separate them, he uses a hyphen to show that the entire group should be included. For example, he might write, "The way Paul told the Ephesians they were to live because they were in God's church is discussed in Ephesians 4-6." The citation tells us that we need to study all of chapters 4, 5, and 6. Use of the hyphen shortens the reference.

Second, a hyphen is used within a specific chapter to show that all of the verses between the first and the second verses listed are included. A writer might say, "Peter's sermon on the day of Pentecost in Jerusalem is found in Acts 2:22-36." The colon tells us we should look in the second chapter of Acts (rule 1). The hyphen tells us that we need to read all of the verses from verse 22 through verse 36 to read Peter's sermon (rule 4). That is a much shorter way to cite all fifteen verses in the sermon than to list each them individually and separate them with commas.

Third, sometimes writers use a hyphen to show that they are referring to all of a passage that begins in one chapter and ends in another chapter. For example, in his Gospel, John tells two stories about people whom Jesus healed. The first is in chapter 4 and is followed immediately by the second which is found in chapter 5. An author might write about the two events this way: "John shows how much Jesus cared for all people in his accounts of the healing of the Roman official's son and of the lame man who walked again (John 4:43-5:9)." The form of the citation tells us that the passage we are to study begins in verse 43 of chapter 4 and continues through verse 9 of chapter 5. As you can tell from that last sentence, the use of the hyphen makes it much easier (and shorter) to say that.

Rule 5: Sometimes, two or more of rules 1-4 will be used to refer to multiple references. For example, a writer may want to refer to a subject or idea that is covered in different verses in different chapters. He might write, "The stories of the signs John recorded to show that Jesus was the Christ, the Son of God (John 20:30-31) are found in John 2:1-11; 4:46-54; 5:1-18; 6:1-14, 16-21; 9:1-4; and 11:1-44." In this example, seven passages in John's Gospel are cited. Several ranges of verses are connected with hyphens. Six different chapters are separated with semi-colons. Two different signs are reported in chapter 6; the first ends in verse 14 and the second begins in verse 16. So a comma is used to separate the reference to the sign in verses 1-14 from the one in verses 16-21.

Rule 6: In addition to the rules that utilize punctuation marks, abbreviations of words are also used. A lower case "v" is used to refer to a single verse of Scripture, as seen in this example: "In Acts 2, Peter told his hearers to repent (v. 38) and 'Save yourselves from this crooked generation' (v. 40)." If the writer intends to refer to more than one verse, he or she may use two "v's", as in, "Luke concludes Acts 2 by reporting on the growth and actions of the earliest church (vv. 42-47)."

The abbreviation "cf." stands for the Latin word *confer* which means "to compare." Many writers use this abbreviation when they want the reader to compare a point made from one passage with another passage of Scripture. For example, one might say, "John's teaching that Jesus existed in the form of God when the world was created (John 1:1-18) is also affirmed by other New Testament writers (cf. Hebrews 1:1-3; Philippians 2:5-11)."

The abbreviation "ff." is a shorter way to refer to verses that follow a cited verse without specifying which verses to consult. For example, we might modify the example we used two paragraphs ago to read, "Luke concludes Acts 2 by reporting on the growth and actions of the earliest church (v. 42ff.)."

A writer may communicate that other passages parallel the one he cites by using the abbreviation "par." as in, "Jesus' feeding of the 5,000 appears in Matthew 14:13-21; par." This abbreviation points to the existence of the parallel texts, but leaves it to the reader to find the specific references (in this case the parallels are Mark 6:32-44; Luke 9:10-17; John 6:1-15).

Abbreviations that are commonly used in other disciplines of study are also employed in writings about the Bible. Citations of dates for events that occurred before the birth of Jesus are indicated by the use of BC (before Christ). AD (Anno Domini, Latin for "in the year of [our] Lord") is used for dating events that occurred after his birth.[1] When a date given is only approximately known, the abbreviation "ca." (from the Latin *circa*, which means about or approximately) is used.

"For example" may be abbreviated as "e.g." (Latin, *exempli gratia*). "Especially" may be shortened to "esp." "And others" is often indicated with et. al. (Latin, *et. alii*). "Etc." means *et cetera*, "and the rest." The abbreviation "i.e." (*id est*) means "that is," a way to designate a specific example of something. (Example: "The first president of the United States, i.e.,

---

[1] In recent years, some have begun to use the abbreviations BCE ("Before Common Era") and CE ("Common Era") in place of BC and AD. For a comment about this change and the rationale for the use of BC and AD in this book, see Note 1 on page 126.

George Washington, established many traditions for the office that are still followed today.")

Bible Book Abbreviations

Instead of writing out the full name of a Bible book—as I have done up to this point—writers often abbreviate book names. Different writers (and publishers) use different abbreviations for some of the books, but the following are fairly standard (and variations of them are not hard to understand).

Old Testament		New Testament
Genesis - Gen	Jeremiah - Jer	Matthew - Matt
Exodus - Exod	Lamentations - Lam	Mark - Mark
Leviticus - Lev	Ezekiel - Ezek	Luke - Luke
Numbers - Num	Daniel - Dan	John - John
Deuteronomy - Deut	Hosea - Hos	Acts - Acts
Joshua - Josh	Joel - Joel	Romans - Rom
Judges - Judg	Amos - Amos	1, 2 Corinthians -
Ruth - Ruth	Obadiah - Obad	1, 2 Cor
1, 2 Samuel - 1, 2 Sam	Jonah - Jon	Galatians - Gal
1, 2 Kings - 1, 2 Kings	Micah - Mic	Ephesians - Eph
1, 2 Chronicles -	Nahum - Nah	Philippians - Phil
1, 2 Chron	Habakkuk - Hab	Colossians - Col
Ezra - Ezra	Zephaniah - Zeph	1, 2 Thessalonians -
Nehemiah - Neh	Haggai - Hag	1, 2 Thess
Esther - Esth	Zechariah - Zech	1, 2 Timothy - 1, 2 Tim
Job - Job	Malachi - Mal	Titus - Tit
Psalms -		Philemon - Phlm
Ps (one chapter)		Hebrews - Heb
Pss (two or more)		James - Jas
Proverbs - Prov		1, 2 Peter - 1, 2 Pet
Ecclesiastes - Eccl		1, 2, 3 John -
Song of Solomon -		1, 2, 3 John
Song		Jude - Jude
Isaiah - Isa		Revelation - Rev

Practice Exercises

Part 1: Convert the following abbreviated references into written statements of what is being abbreviated.

Example: John 21:12 — John, chapter twenty-one, verse twelve

1. Isa 43, 45, 59, 61 —
2. Deut 6:4-5, 7, 12-14 —
3. Jer 31:23; 25:27-31 —
4. Rom 6:23-7:14 —
5. Dan 6:1-7 —
6. Gen 3:15; Exod 3:6; Lev 16:20 —
7. Rev 12-16 —
8. Acts 2; 3:5-7, 18; 5:1-11 —
9. 2 Tim 3:14-4:5 —
10. Jon 1, 3, 4 —

Part 2: For each of the following, convert the written statement to an abbreviation, as in the example.

Example: Isaiah, chapter seven, verses 14 through 16 — Isa 7:14-16

1. First Corinthians, chapters seven, nine, eleven, verses 10 through 12 —

2. Job, chapter six, verse 3 through chapter seven, verse 5, and chapter 12 —

3. Psalm, chapter 13, verses six through eight, and eleven —

4. Malachi, chapters 2 and 3, and Matthew, chapters 2 and 4.

5. Romans, chapter two, verses 21 through 26, chapter 3, verses one through seven, chapter 6, verse 4, chapter fourteen, verses 1 through 20.

Section 2: Surveying the Bible's Story

CHAPTER 4

The Bible's Grand Story

YOU MAY RECALL FROM chapter 1 that one of the differences between the Bible and other books we read is that it tells a different *story*. The sixty-six Bible books were written over a time period covering about 1,500 years. As we will see, its main story begins when God called Abraham and includes events that took place over about 2,000 years. Yet, from beginning to end —Genesis to Revelation—the Bible tells one grand story.

To review our brief summary from chapter 1, the Bible tells the story of God versus evil. More specifically, it tells how God took the initiative to enact his plan to deliver people from sin and its effects so we can have the opportunity to experience the close relationship with him that people enjoyed right after creation. Restoration, or reconciliation (becoming friends again), is necessary because sin fractures our relationship with God. The Bible uses several words to describe the result of God's initiative and plan, including "deliver," "rescue," and "redeem." But the primary word it uses is "salvation." In light of the Bible's story, we can say that salvation is God's action to rescue people from the consequences of sin.

Jesus himself endorsed the idea that the Bible is telling one story. In two places in Luke 24, he explained the meaning of his crucifixion and resurrection to his disciples. He said that it was "necessary that the Christ should suffer these things and enter into his glory." Luke then said that Jesus began with "Moses and all the Prophets" and "interpreted . . . in all the Scriptures the things concerning himself" (Luke 24:26-27). Later in the chapter, Jesus repeated the explanation about his suffering and said things had to be that way because "everything written about me in the Law of Moses and the Prophets and the Psalms must be fulfilled." Luke then added that "he opened their minds to understand the Scriptures" (vv. 44-46).

As we saw in chapter 1 (see Additional Note 2, p. 22), "Moses and all the Prophets" and "the Law of Moses and the Prophets and the Psalms" were phrases used by the Jewish people to refer to all of the books that Christians refer to as the Old Testament. Jesus was saying that his crucifixion and resurrection were bringing to completion the story that was being told throughout those writings. This is the Bible's grand story.

A Panoramic View

Remember the scene on the puzzle box we envisioned in chapter 1? It was a view across a prairie field of wheat with snow-capped mountains in the background, a scene of a vast landscape under a blue sky dotted by several small clouds. We didn't focus on single blades of wheat growing on the prairie, or how sharp the edges of some of the rocks on the mountainside might be. We were looking only at the big picture.

Although we will be looking more closely at the different parts of it, we are approaching the Bible's story the same way in the next five chapters. In this chapter, we will survey it as a whole. In chapters 5-8, we will narrow our focus to look at the major events in the story's various historical periods.

Before we begin, however, I need to tell you how I am using the words "story" and "grand."

A "Grand Story"?

According to the web site, dictionary.com, the noun "story" has *ten* meanings.[1] One definition is "a lie or fabrication," that is, a made-up story. Other meanings refer to the plot of a short story, novel, play, or movie, etc., or some other "fictitious tale." The word may also be used to refer to a story that need not be true but is told to entertain or make a point, such as an anecdote or a joke. When we read those definitions, we might think of fairy tales that begin with the words, "once upon a time."

Because there are skeptics who question whether the events in the Bible really occurred, some have said that using the word "story" to talk about the Bible's narrative leaves the impression that we do not think the events really happened. I understand that concern since, as we have seen, "story" does sometimes refer to made-up or false accounts. It is even used sometimes to refer to one person's view of reality that might not match the perceptions of someone else.

But we should also consider other meanings of "story" in the dictionary's list. The first definition says that a story is "a narrative, either *true* or fictitious, . . ." (emphasis mine). Another definition adds that "story" is sometimes used in the sense of a "news story" which reports something that occurred. A third meaning refers to "a narration of the events in the life of a person or the existence of a thing, or such events as a subject for narration: [as in] the story of medicine; the story of his life." In each of these definitions, "story" is used to refer to events that are believed to have really occurred.

I am using this meaning when I refer to the *story* the Bible tells. In truth, many Christian people have used "story" this way for a long time, as illustrated in the hymns, "Tell Me the Story of Jesus," written in 1880 by Fanny J. Crosby, and "O Listen to Our Wondrous Story," written by James M. Gray in

---

[1] *Dictionary.com*, s.v. "Story," accessed June 7, 2018, http://dictionary.reference.com/. The authors note that "history," the tenth meaning listed, is obsolete.

1903. When I speak of the Bible's story, I mean to refer to the narrative of real events in which God was advancing his plan to save people from the consequences of sin.

That story is indeed "grand." Unlike the word "story," in which we are focusing on just one of several meanings, multiple meanings of the word "grand" fit what we see in the Bible's story. It is "impressive in size, appearance, or general effect." It is "stately, majestic, or dignified." It is "magnificent or splendid" and "noble or revered." Furthermore, its goal is "highly ambitious or idealistic."[2] Simply stated, the Bible is telling *God's* story as he reached out to sinful people to rescue us from our sin and restore us to the kind of relationship with him that Adam and Eve enjoyed in the garden of Eden.

Why We Need Salvation

The first words in the Bible are, "In the beginning" (Gen 1:1). The first eleven chapters of Genesis present a reasonable explanation of the origin of the universe and sin. Genesis 1-2 are concerned with the origin of people, and in particular with the close relationship the first humans had with God in a created world that Scripture describes as "very good" (Gen 1:31). These chapters also present ideals for how people were intended to live and relate to one another (cf. Gen 2:24; Matt 19:6).

Genesis 3-11 show where things went wrong and then became worse. Genesis 3 tells how Adam and Eve gave in to temptation with the result that sin became a regular feature of life in the world. Nothing was ever the same again. Because of sin, Adam and Eve were separated from God and faced the prospect of death (cf. Gen 2:17; 3:14-24). What is worse, everyone else chose the same path. Genesis 4 tells the story of the couple's oldest son, Cain, murdering his brother, Abel. By the beginning of Genesis 6, "the wickedness of man" had become so bad "that every intention of the thoughts of his heart

2 *Dictionary.com*, s.v. "Grand," accessed June 7, 2018, http://dictionary.reference.com/.

was only evil continually" (6:5). Because of this, God sent a great flood on the world. He spared only Noah and his family because Noah demonstrated faith in God (cf. Heb 11:7). But, sadly, this cleansing of the world didn't last. Sin continued as people kept trying to be "like God" and "make a name for [themselves]" (Gen 3:5; 11:4) instead of revering God's name and obeying his commands.

A Man, Then a Nation

Genesis 12 is a turning point and where the story of salvation properly begins. After the flood, God chose a descendant of Shem, one of Noah's sons, to be the man through whom he would bring reconciliation to everyone. At the time God called him, the man's name was Abram; it was later changed to Abraham (Gen 17:5; I will refer to him as Abraham from here on). At the time of his call, God told him how he fit into the plan.

> [1] Now the LORD said to Abram, "Go from your country and your kindred and your father's house to the land that I will show you. [2] And I will make of you a great nation, and I will bless you and make your name great, so that you will be a blessing. [3] I will bless those who bless you, and him who dishonors you I will curse, and in you all the families of the earth shall be blessed."
> . . . [7] Then the LORD appeared to Abram and said, "To your offspring I will give this land." So he built there an altar to the LORD, who had appeared to him (Gen 12:1-3, 7).

In these verses, we learn that God chose Abraham for a purpose and made great promises to him. He said that he would both receive God's blessing and be a blessing to others. Even though he and his wife Sarai (later called Sarah) had no children at the time, God told him that his descendants would one day be "a great nation." But this would not happen just to make Abraham famous, or for the nation's own sake. God told Abraham he was being chosen to "be a blessing" to others (v. 2) and then added that in Abraham, "all the families of the earth shall be blessed."

It is important to understand two other things about this promise. First, seeing that the primary focus of God's promise was on Abraham and his descendants being a blessing to others is necessary in order to correctly understand the part of the promise about the land that Abraham's descendants would receive. When God called him, Abraham's home was in "Ur of the Chaldeans" (Babylon) (cf. Gen 11:28, 31). God told him to go "the land that I will show you" (Gen 12:1).[3] After he arrived in that land, which was then known as Canaan (vv. 4-6), "the LORD appeared to Abram and said, 'To your offspring I will give this land'" (v. 7). That land would later be the physical location of the nation inhabited by the descendants God promised to Abraham. Both the nation and land would be known as "Israel," and the land would be a special place for God's people. But as stated in Genesis 12, the land was part of the larger plan for Abraham's descendants to exist so that all the earth's families would be blessed.

Second, notice that Genesis 12:7 uses the singular noun, "offspring." Some translations use the plural form of the word here (RSV; NASB; NKJV), no doubt to harmonize it with the rest of the promise's emphasis on the *many* descendants Abraham would have. But the Hebrew word for "descendant" in the verse is singular in number (as translated in the KJV; ASV; NIV; NRSV; and ESV). As we will see in more detail in chapter 5, Paul would later interpret the significance of Jesus by emphasizing that Genesis 12 uses the singular form of the word. His point was that Jesus was the one "offspring" who was sent to fulfill the promise God made to Abraham (Gal 3:16).

---

[3] The locations mentioned here were within the Fertile Crescent which included the Nile River valley in Egypt, the plains along the Mediterranean coast of Palestine, and the Tigris and Euphrates river valleys. Since rainfall in those areas was sufficient to support agriculture, the earliest Near Eastern civilizations developed there. The city of Babylon, on the eastern side of the crescent, became the center of power in two periods: Old Babylon (ca. 2000-1600 BC), and Neo-Babylon (ca. 600-550 BC). Abraham lived at the time of the Old Babylonian era.

As the story unfolds throughout the rest of Genesis and first part of Exodus, God eventually blessed Abraham and Sarah with a son named Isaac. He in turn was the father of twin sons, Esau and Jacob, the second of whom carried on the blessing and plan of God. Jacob, whose name was changed to "Israel" (Gen 32:28), became the father of twelve sons who became the ancestors of the people in the nation of Israel. The nation was divided into twelve groups, or "tribes," each named after one of the sons.

The eleventh son, Joseph, was sold into slavery by his brothers and taken to Egypt. The wife of Potiphar, his Egyptian master, made false accusations against him and Potiphar had him imprisoned. But because God granted him the ability to interpret dreams, Joseph was able to warn Pharaoh about a coming famine and tell him how to prepare for it. Pharaoh gave him authority as Egypt's second most powerful man and Joseph led the nation in storing grain throughout seven plentiful years to prepare for the seven years of famine that were coming (cf. Gen 37, 39-50).

The famine afflicted both Egypt and Canaan during the last part of Jacob's life. He sent Joseph's brothers to Egypt to buy food and, after reuniting with Joseph, the entire family moved there. Initially, they and their descendants were treated well, but a later Egyptian ruler considered them a threat and enslaved them (Exod 1:8-22). Through the leadership of Moses, God delivered them from slavery and began to lead them toward Canaan, the land he had promised to give to Abraham's chosen descendants (Exod 3-14). The Bible says that a census taken in the second year after they left Egypt revealed that Jacob's family had grown from seventy people (Gen 46:27) to 603,500 men who were twenty years old and older (Num 1:45-46). An additional 22,000 Levite males a month old and older were not counted with the other tribes (Num 3:39). In terms of population, Abraham's descendants had grown to the size of a nation.

Three months after they left Egypt, God gave Moses the law that would govern them (Exod 20:1-17). Before giving them the commandments, however, he reminded them of the calling and purpose he had originally declared to Abraham.

> ¹ On the third new moon after the people of Israel had gone out of the land of Egypt, on that day they came into the wilderness of Sinai. ² They set out from Rephidim and came into the wilderness of Sinai, and they encamped in the wilderness. There Israel encamped before the mountain, ³ while Moses went up to God. The LORD called to him out of the mountain, saying, "Thus you shall say to the house of Jacob, and tell the people of Israel: ⁴'You yourselves have seen what I did to the Egyptians, and how I bore you on eagles' wings and brought you to myself. ⁵ Now therefore, if you will indeed obey my voice and keep my covenant, you shall be my treasured possession among all peoples, for all the earth is mine; ⁶ and you shall be to me a kingdom of priests and a holy nation.' These are the words that you shall speak to the people of Israel" (Exod 19:1-6).

Three things are especially important in these verses for understanding the Bible's story. First, verse 4 emphasizes that it was by grace that God had chosen them as a people and delivered them from their Egyptian masters. Second, in verse 5, he told them that he had chosen them to be his "treasured possession among all peoples." Third, in verses 5 and 6, he told them that they were expected to "obey [his] voice and keep [his] covenant" and that in doing so they would be "a kingdom of priests and a holy nation." The point of these statements was to emphasize that Israel had been selected to show other nations how to revere and obey God. In other words, they existed as a nation so that they could be a blessing to others.

Moving Forward Despite Many Detours

If we were to depict the progress of God's story with a map of a highway, we would not draw a wide, straight expressway free of traffic jams. Instead, the road would be a narrow, crooked mountain road with detours along the way to get around the obstructions caused by falling rocks. Those obstacles slow, but do not stop the journey. They are incorporated into the navigation as progress continues toward the destination.

For Israel, the detours began before they reached the promised land. Lack of faith and a refusal to trust God resulted in the journey to Canaan taking forty years instead of just a few months. Despite the setbacks, God led them to the border of the land. Under the leadership of Joshua, he enabled them to conquer and settle in it. They did not live "happily ever after" in their new home, however. Just as their ancestors had done in the wilderness, they turned to the gods worshiped by the people around them instead of following God alone (cf. Josh 24:14; Exod 32:1-6). This choice led them to practice the same kind of evil behavior that their neighbors practiced. Examples of their sin and the troubles it caused are found in the book of Judges (cf. Judg 17:6; 21:25).

In time, their desire to be like the other nations led the people to ask for a king. God granted their request and three men ruled over the united nation. In order, they were Saul, David, and Solomon. But national unity lasted just 120 years. Under Rehoboam, Solomon's son and successor, ten of the twelve tribes broke away to form their own nation. The new nation became known as Israel and the nation that remained with Rehoboam was called Judah.

The history of both nations followed the same path of departure from God and his law, although the departure took longer in Judah than in Israel. God sent multiple prophets to warn and urge them to turn back to him, but most of the people refused to listen (cf. Isa 6:9-13; Hos 4:16; Zech 7:11). Finally, God allowed both Israel and Judah to be conquered by foreign powers, conquests that enacted his judgment on them for not remaining faithful to his covenant with them (cf. Exod 19:5). Israel was defeated by Assyria; Judah was conquered by Neo-Babylon and the majority of the people were exiled. Even before their defeat, however, God promised that a part of them, a remnant, would return to their land (cf. Isa 10:20-22; 11:11, 16; 28:5; 37:31-32). The nation's glory would be restored and its mission to be an example and blessing to others would continue. In spite of Israel's unfaithfulness, the promise that God would work through them to bless all nations would proceed toward its fulfillment.

We see evidence of this hope in passages in the Psalms and the Prophets. We will illustrate it from Isaiah. Especially in chapters 40-66, Isaiah emphasized that even though it appeared that the Babylonian exile meant the end for Israel, God's plan would still succeed because he is sovereign over both the creation and history. Israel would once again be a positive example to the other nations and the means by which all peoples would be blessed. Furthermore, a designated servant of the Lord would one day arrive to deliver God's people and provide the way for other nations to be included in the promise first made to Abraham.

We will focus on just two of the passages in Isaiah that demonstrate this hope. Isaiah 42:1-9 speaks of the coming of the Lord's "servant," the one he would "uphold" as his "chosen, in whom [his] soul delights." Furthermore, God would "put [his] Spirit upon him" (v. 1). The servant's mission would be to "bring forth justice to the nations" (vv. 1, 3-4), and "the coastlands [would] wait for his law" (v. 4). In the time of Isaiah, "coastlands" was a word that referred to the lands around the Mediterranean Sea. Isaiah's reference to them was a way of saying that the servant's work would benefit people in places far removed from physical Israel's location at the eastern end of the Mediterranean. Verse 6 spells out the role and mission of the servant. "I will give you as a covenant for the people, a light for the nations" (cf. Isa 49:6).

Isaiah 61:1-11 announces a similar message. The word "servant" does not appear in this passage, but it is commonly understood that he is its subject. He said, "The Spirit of the Lord GOD is upon me, because the LORD has anointed me to bring good news to the poor; he has sent me to bind up the brokenhearted, to proclaim liberty to the captives, and the opening of the prison to those who are bound" (v. 1). His mission would be "to proclaim the year of the LORD'S favor, to comfort all who mourn" (v. 2). The people who would be restored to favor were told that they would one day "be called priests of the LORD" and "eat the wealth of the nations" (vv. 6, 10; cf. Exod 19:6). Furthermore, "their offspring shall be known among the nations" (v. 9) with the result that "the Lord GOD will cause righteousness and praise to sprout up before all the nations" (v. 11).

These passages illustrate the expectation, seen throughout the Old Testament, that a time would come when God would fulfill his promise to bless all peoples through Abraham's descendants. But as the Old Testament ends, the story is incomplete.

The Rest of the Story

As we begin to read the New Testament, we discover a sense of longing for the fulfillment of the promises made to Abraham and reinforced through the prophets. We see it immediately in the first seventeen verses of Matthew, the first book of the New Testament. Verse 1 tells us that the book is going to be concerned with "Jesus Christ." But that verse also presents the life of Jesus against the background of God's promises. Matthew said that Jesus was "the son of David, the son of Abraham" (Matt 1:1). Verses 2-16 trace his ancestry from Abraham to David (vv. 2-6), from David to the beginning of the Babylonian exile (vv. 7-11), and then from the exile to Joseph and Mary (vv. 12-16). Verse 17 summarizes, "So all the generations from Abraham to David were fourteen generations, and from David to the deportation to Babylon fourteen generations, and from the deportation to Babylon to the Christ fourteen generations." Throughout his Gospel, Matthew continued to emphasize that everything Jesus did and said was to fulfill the promises that began with Abraham and continued through the lineage of King David and the announcements of the prophets (see the word "fulfill" in Matt 1:22; 2:15, 17, 23; 3:15; 4:14; 5:17; 8:17; 12:17; 13:35; 21:4; 26:54, 56; 27:9).

Mark, Luke, and John also show how Jesus was completing the story that began in the Old Testament. Because Luke continued his account in Acts, we will look at selected passages from both books to illustrate the story's ongoing progress in the ministry of Jesus and activities of the first Christians.

First, notice Simeon's encounter with Mary and Joseph when they took the infant Jesus to the temple in Jerusalem for his purification (Luke 2:21-22). Simeon was a righteous man who was "waiting for the consolation of Israel" (Luke 2:25). The word "consolation" was the same word used in the Greek translation of passages in Isaiah that promised that God would one day rescue and "comfort" his people (cf. Isa 40:1-2, 11; 49:13; 61:2; 66:13).

Luke 2:26 explains that the reason Simeon approached Joseph and Mary that day was because "it had been revealed to him by the Holy Spirit that he would not see death before he had seen the Lord's Christ," or "Messiah" (NRSV; "Christ" is the English translation of the Greek word which was used to translate the Hebrew word for "Messiah"). Jesus was the one for whom the Israelites had been waiting. Simeon took the baby in his arms and said, "my eyes have seen your *salvation. . .* prepared in the presence of all *peoples*" (vv. 30-31). Then, he added that the baby he held was the servant who had been promised in Isaiah, the one who would be "a light for revelation to the Gentiles ["nations" in Isaiah], and for glory to your people Israel" (v. 32; cf. Isa 42:6; 49:6).

Simeon was saying that Jesus was completing the story that had been developing throughout the Old Testament. He was the "offspring" (cf. Gen 12:3; Gal. 3:16) promised to Abraham, the one through whom all nations would be blessed.

We turn next to Luke 4:18-21. Jesus had gone to Nazareth where he had grown up and was given the opportunity to address the people in the synagogue on the Sabbath. According to synagogue custom, he was given the scroll of the prophet Isaiah which he opened to what we know as chapter 61:1-2. He read the passage and then said, "Today, this Scripture has been fulfilled in your hearing" (Luke 4:21). Jesus was claiming that he was the servant depicted in Isaiah 61 (see above). He then went on to say that, in his mission, God intended to bless people outside the nation of Israel (cf. vv. 25-27). As his ministry proceeded, Jesus demonstrated that he was the expected servant by welcoming people who were social outcasts. These people were disregarded or thought to be of lesser value and importance by those who considered themselves to be faithful keepers of the ways of God's law (cf. Luke 15:1-2). Jesus welcomed people who were blind, lame, lepers, and the poor, the people the prophets had said would be blessed by the Lord's servant when God visited Israel to keep his promises to "the nations" (cf. Isa 35:4-10; Luke 7:18-23).

The third passage in Luke we will notice is his report on Jesus' transfiguration. Luke's account is more detailed than the ones found in the parallel passages in Matthew and Mark. Only in Luke do we learn what Jesus talked about with Moses and Elijah when they appeared with him on the mountain. Luke 9:31 says that all of them "appeared in glory and spoke of his *departure*, which he was about to *accomplish* in Jerusalem" (cf. Matt 17:3; Mark 9:4). In the Greek text, the word "accomplish" is the word that is often translated "fulfill" (see the NIV). But a more important word in the verse is "departure," a translation of the Greek word *exodos*. Like Israel of old, Jesus was going to experience an "exodus" on the way to being glorified. In this way, he would "fulfill," or "accomplish" God's work to bring salvation and reconciliation to all people. In his service, Jesus was bringing the grand story to its climax.

Luke's second volume, Acts, continues the story. Jesus told his followers to spread the news of forgiveness and salvation to all the nations (Luke 24:47-48; Acts 1:8). As they told the story of Jesus, his followers made sure to connect it with the events of the Old Testament. For example, after Peter healed a lame man in the temple (Acts 3:1-10), he told Jesus' story to the crowd that gathered. He explicitly connected Jesus' work to the God of Abraham, Isaac, Jacob, and the fathers (Acts 3:13). He identified Jesus as God's "servant," using the same word that was used in the Greek translation of the servant passages in Isaiah (Acts 3:13; cf. Isa 42:1; 49:6; 52:13). He said that Jesus' suffering had been expected by the prophets (Acts 3:18), and that his work was the culmination of God's plan to "restore all the things" spoken by the "prophets long ago" (v. 21). Jesus was the expected "prophet like Moses" (v. 22; cf. Deut 18:15, 18-19), and the things he was doing had been declared by the prophets, evidence that God was completing the agreement (covenant) he had made with Abraham. Peter then quoted Genesis 12:3 to conclude his address, saying, "You are the sons of the prophets and of the covenant that God made with your fathers, saying to Abraham, '*And in your offspring shall all the families of the earth be blessed*'" (v. 25).

Paul also said that the story begun in the Old Testament was being completed in the service of Jesus' followers. Although he emphasized different parts of the Old Testament accounts, his synagogue sermon at Antioch of Pisidia told the story in essentially the same way Peter had told it in Acts 2 and 3. He surveyed Israel's history, referring especially to events related to God's promises; called attention to Jesus' death and resurrection; and stressed that Jesus was the "offspring" (Acts 13:23) whom God had sent to fulfill the messianic promises made to David and declared by the prophets (Acts 13:16-41). Many wanted to hear Paul speak again about those things, but some jealous Jewish leaders saw the crowds that had assembling and began to contradict him (vv. 42-45). Paul then told them he was turning to the Gentiles.

> [46] And Paul and Barnabas spoke out boldly, saying, "It was necessary that the word of God be spoken first to you. Since you thrust it aside and judge yourselves unworthy of eternal life, behold, we are turning to the Gentiles. [47] For so the Lord has commanded us, saying, 'I have made you a light for the Gentiles, that you may bring salvation to the ends of the earth.'" [48] And when the Gentiles heard this, they began rejoicing and glorifying the word of the Lord, and as many as were appointed to eternal life believed (Acts 13:46-48).

In words similar to Simeon's in Luke 2:32, Paul defended taking the good news to the Gentiles by quoting Isaiah's declaration that God's servant would be "a light to the Gentiles [nations]." He also quoted the phrase that promised the servant would "bring salvation to the ends of the earth" (Acts 13:47; cf. Isa 49:6). Later, to King Agrippa, he made the same defense for taking the good news to the Gentiles, emphasizing that the prophets and Moses had spoken of Christ's suffering (Acts 26:23; cf. Isa 42:6; 49:6). In presenting the message that way, Paul joined the consistent testimony of the entire New Testament in saying that the story begun with Abraham was being completed by followers of Jesus.

Conclusion

In recent years, the internet has made it easier for us to research our ancestry. As a result, the search for family roots has become increasingly popular. At least part of the reason for the widespread interest in tracing family history is that we all want to feel we are part of something bigger than ourselves, something that goes beyond the brief span of our natural lives.

We can be part of nothing greater than the grand story God has unfolded throughout history. When we turn to him, we become part of the story that began with promises to Abraham, reached fulfillment in the service of Jesus, and continues even now through the work of his church.

For Review and Thought

1. Show from Luke 24 how Jesus endorsed the idea that the Bible is telling one story.
2. "Moses and all the Prophets." "The Law of Moses and the Prophets and the Psalms." Why are these phrases significant?
3. What possible problem is there with using the word "story" to refer to the Bible's narratives? Explain how the word is being used in this chapter.
4. In what way is the Bible's story "grand"?
5. What beginnings do we find in Genesis 1-2?
6. In view of Genesis 3-11, explain why we need salvation.
7. In what passage does the Bible's story of rescue really begin? Who was chosen for a special role in the story? What promises did God make to him?
8. Explain why Jacob's family went to Egypt, what happened to them there, and why we can say they had become a "nation" when they left.
9. Identify the three ideas from Exodus 19:1-6 that are especially important for understanding the Bible's story.
10. What were the "obstacles" and "detours" God's plan had to overcome as Israel lived in the land?
11. Explain the importance of the following terms as used in Isaiah: the Lord's servant; coastlands; and nations.
12. How do the first seventeen verses in the New Testament show that the story begun in the Old Testament was continuing?
13. Explain why the following ideas in these passages from Luke are important for understanding the ongoing story: [a] the consolation of Israel; the Lord's Christ; salvation; a light for the nations; Gentiles (2:25-32); [b] "Today, this Scripture has been fulfilled in your hearing" (4:21); [c] departure; accomplish (9:31).
14. In Acts 3, how did Peter connect Jesus to the Old Testament story and show that it was continuing?
15. Identify the passages in Acts where Paul cited Isaiah 42:6 and 49:6. How did his citations offer a defense for his ministry? What do his citations show he thought about the Bible's story?
16. Explain the significance of this statement: "We can be part of nothing greater than the grand story God has unfolded throughout history."

CHAPTER 5

Creation to Occupation

As WE STUDY ANY part of the Bible, whether a complete book or a specific passage, it is important to keep in mind where it fits in the big picture of the whole story. Dividing the story into historical divisions, with headlines that highlight its major developments, provides a framework that makes it easier to keep track of the many events reported in Scripture. I encourage you to learn the list of fourteen historical divisions used here or one like it (see the chart, p. 80). You might even want to adopt the practice of a teacher I once knew and review the divisions every time you begin a study of a Bible book or section. This will not only reinforce your memory of the historical periods, it will also help you see where the specific part of the Bible you are studying fits in the larger story.

Determining and Recording Dates

Before beginning the survey of the divisions, we should think about how dates for ancient events are determined. Ancient writers (in and out of the Bible) recorded dates differently from the way they are written now. To illustrate, compare the modern citation of June 6, 1944, the date American history students know as D-Day in Normandy, with how it would have been written in antiquity. A reference written in the style used by ancient writers would read something like this: "D-Day in France occurred in the fourth year after Germany began World War II by invading Poland. This was during Winston S. Churchill's first term as prime minister of Great Britain, during the last year of the U. S. presidency of Franklin D. Roosevelt."

We see similar wording in Scripture. For example, 1 Kings 15:1 says that, after the death of King Rehoboam, "in the eighteenth year of King Jeroboam the son of Nebat, Abijam began to reign over Judah." The book of Amos says that it was reporting things the prophet "saw concerning Israel in the days of Uzziah king of Judah and in the days of Jeroboam the son of Joash, king of Israel, two years before the earthquake" (Amos 1:1). The Gospel of Luke says that Joseph and Mary went to Bethlehem for the birth of Jesus at the time of "the first registration when Quirinius was governor of Syria" (Luke 2:1). In the next chapter, Luke wrote that the ministry of John the Baptist began "in the fifteenth year of the reign of Tiberius Caesar" (3:1).

Notice that ancient date references typically did not specify an exact month and day, or even give the number for a specific year. Yet, as we read modern accounts of ancient events, including those mentioned in the Bible, we routinely see references to specific years (for example, the fall of Jerusalem in 586 BC). Since ancient writers were not as specific in recording dates as we are, how can modern writers be so confident in giving specific dates for ancient events?

Their confidence is possible because of the work in analyzing the evidence that has been done by archaeologists, astronomers, and historians. Ancient civilizations including the Egyptians, Babylonians, Assyrians, Greeks, and Romans, had developed calendars. Lists of kings and how long they reigned were common in the ancient Near East. Kings and other public figures ensured that their accomplishments were recorded, often in inscriptions on temples, public buildings, statues, and similar objects. The discovery of those inscriptions has provided much information about the ancient world.

Often, ancient records referred to events that occurred in year x of the reign of King Y, or in relation to a notable natural event, like an earthquake (see Amos 1:1) or solar eclipse. Scholars compare the records from the different empires (such as Assyria, Babylon, and Egypt) to identify overlapping references to events. Some events can be dated with more precision and become important markers for calculating timelines backward and forward to other events.[1]

The timeline that results from this analysis is how we can say with assurance that Amos saw his vision in about 760 BC, that Jerusalem fell in 586 BC, that Jesus was born in about 5 BC, and that John began his ministry in about 27 or 28 AD. References to the dates are generally not as precise as modern references to D-Day in France, the end of Winston Churchill's first term as prime minister (July 26, 1945), or the death of Franklin Roosevelt (April 12, 1945). But it is possible to assign dates to ancient events within relatively small windows of time.

The dates given in the surveys that follow are widely accepted by students of ancient history. Generally, dates from the beginning of Israel's United Kingdom period through the

---

[1] Surviving king lists and official year-by-year archive records from the Assyrian and Neo-Babylonian empires are especially helpful for determining the dates for the kings of Israel and Judah in the Divided Kingdom Period. For example, the Assyrian king Sennacherib invaded Judah during the reign of Hezekiah (1 Kings 18:13-19:36). We know that Sennacherib ruled from 705-681 BC. From his annals, notably the six-sided Taylor (or Sennacherib) Prism discovered in 1830 in the ruins in Nineveh, historians are able to date Assyria's invasion of Judah in 701. First Kings 18:13 says the invasion was "in the fourteenth year of King Hezekiah," whose name is mentioned on the Taylor Prism. From this, we can date the beginning of Hezekiah's reign in 715.

The work of astronomers helps us have even more confidence. An inscription dated in the tenth year of the Assyrian king, Ashur-dan III, refers to a solar eclipse that astronomers have determined occurred June 15, 763 BC. That calculation, along with other references to astronomical events, inscriptions, and other records from Assyria and elsewhere, allows historians to work backward and forward from 763. The result is a reliable chronology for the first millennium BC.

end of the New Testament era are more firmly established than dates in the previous periods. With regard to Old Testament events, this confidence comes from knowing about the solar eclipse in Assyria in 763 BC, the event that serves as the marker for establishing dates before and after 763 (see note [1]). Scholars are generally confident about the chronology back to about 1000 BC, but the chronology of the third and second millennia BC is not so firmly established.

A question about which there has been much debate is when Israel's exodus from Egypt occurred. Related to that question are the matters of determining the dates of the patriarchs before the exodus and the time of the judges afterward. Two views are proposed among scholars who believe firmly that the Bible was "breathed out by God" (2 Tim 3:16). Proponents of the early view believe the exodus occurred in the 15th century BC (1400s). Those who support the late view believe it happened in the 13th century (1200s). Defenders of both views support their conclusions with appeals to passages of Scripture and discoveries by archaeologists.

For the purposes of this survey, I am listing the *approximate dates* favored by proponents of the early view in the section headings (dates corresponding to the late view are included in the chart on p. 80). I also use the abbreviation, "ca." (for the Latin *circa*, around or about) with the dates of the periods prior to the United Kingdom to indicate that there is less certainty about those dates. That abbreviation also serves as a reminder that the purpose of listing any dates is to provide a framework for the story, along with an appreciation for how long it took God to complete his plan.

1. From Creation to Abraham
Genesis 1-11 (?? - ca. 2095 BC)

As we saw in chapter 4, before the Bible begins to tell the story of God's work to save people from sin through the promises made to Abraham, it shows how everything came into existence and why salvation is needed. In effect, Genesis 1-11 is the introduction to the story of God's plan. These eleven chapters can be divided into two sections.

Genesis 1:1-2:25 explains the origin of all that exists by saying that God acted to create all things. Chapter 1 surveys the entire creation project. Genesis 2 focuses on the creation of humans, identified in 1:26-27 as the pinnacle of creation. From these chapters we learn that God is a supremely powerful and knowledgeable being who is in control of the world. The word that is often used to describe his control is "sovereignty."

The special place humanity occupies in creation is demonstrated in three ways. First, only after God created people does the Bible say that "everything he had made" was *very good*" (Gen 1:31). Before that, only the word "good" appears at the conclusion of the descriptions of the different days of creation (vv. 4, 10, 12, 18, 21, 25). Second, only humans are said to have been created in God's "image" and "likeness" (v. 26). Third, only humans were given a special responsibility in creation. Twice in chapter 1, God said that people were to "have dominion" over the rest of creation (vv. 26, 28). Plants and animals were created for the benefit of humans (vv. 29-30). Humanity's special place was not intended to be seen merely as a privilege, however. It was a blessing to be used responsibly. People were expected to "work" and to "maintain" (NET) the garden God provided after they were created (Gen 2:15-16). This expectation was in effect before the man and woman sinned (cf. 3:17-19).

At first, Adam and Eve, named as the first man and woman, enjoyed a close relationship with God in a place known as the garden of Eden. As beings created in God's image, they had freedom of choice, the exercise of which had consequences. God told them they could "eat from any tree in the garden" except one. They were not to eat the fruit of "the tree of the knowledge of good and evil" that grew in "the middle of the garden" (Gen 2:16-17; 3:3; NIV). God did not make it impossible for them to eat that fruit, however. Instead, he told them that if they did choose to eat it, the consequence of their choice would be death (Gen 2:17; 3:3). A serpent was the voice of temptation, assuring Eve that they would *not* die if they ate from that tree (Gen 3:1-7). Eve and Adam believed the serpent and chose to eat the forbidden fruit. Because they did not obey God, they were banished from Eden and no longer enjoyed the close relationship with him they once had. Eventually they died, just as God had said (Gen 3:8-24; cf. 5:5).

When Adam and Eve chose to disobey God, they committed the first sin. Once sin entered the world, people continued to choose to sin and became increasingly evil. Genesis 6:7 says that their evil became so bad that God was "sorry" he had made the world. He sent a great flood that destroyed everything except Noah, his family, and the animals that God told Noah to take into the ark that he was to build (Gen 6-8). Sadly, people did not learn from God's judgment and after the flood they continued trying to "be like God" (Gen 3:5). They set out to guide their own lives instead of listening to God's guidance (cf. Jer 10:23). The Bible's introduction concludes with humanity's attempt to build a city with a tower that would reach into the heavens. They did this in an effort to "make a name for" themselves (Gen 11:4).

Genesis 3-11 shows the universal presence of sin. It sets the stage for beginning the story of how God carried out his plan to save people from sin.

2. Patriarchal Period
Genesis 12-50; Job (ca. 2095-1880 BC)

We also noted in chapter 4 that the Bible's primary story begins in Genesis 12:1-7, after the introduction in chapters 1-11. God called Abram (Abraham) and made three promises to him. His descendants would become a great nation, inherit the land that God would show him, and be the people through whom all families of the earth would be blessed.

> [1] Now the LORD said to Abram, "Go from your country and your kindred and your father's house to the land that I will show you. [2] And I will make of you a great nation, and I will bless you and make your name great, so that you will be a blessing. [3] I will bless those who bless you, and him who dishonors you I will curse, and in you all the families of the earth shall be blessed."
>
> . . . [7] Then the LORD appeared to Abram and said, "To your offspring I will give this land." So he built there an altar to the LORD, who had appeared to him.

We gain better understanding of these promises, especially the third one, from New Testament passages that look back on them. In the second recorded sermon in Acts, Peter referred to the blessing that would come to all the earth's families (cf. Acts 3:13, 25). In his epistle to the Romans, Paul taught that the promise to Abraham was not restricted to his physical descendants in Israel, but extended to all people who practiced the kind of faith that Abraham demonstrated, whether they were Jews or Gentiles (cf. Rom 4:13, 16). In his epistle to the Galatians, Paul noted the significance of the singular noun "offspring" in the part of the promise recorded in Genesis 12:7, "To your *offspring* I will give this land." Paul wrote, "Now the promises were made to Abraham and to his offspring. *It does not say, 'and to offsprings,' referring to many, but referring to one, 'and to your offspring,' who is Christ*" (Gal 3:16).[2]

Abraham needed great faith because it was many years after God called him before he saw the fulfillment of even the first of the promises. He was 75 years old when God called him, but the heir through whom the promises would be fulfilled was not born until he was 100 (cf. Gen 12:4; 17:17, 19; 18:10; 21:3). That son, Isaac, became the father of twin sons, Esau and Jacob. As the oldest, Esau normally would have been the heir, but since he was short-sighted, sexually immoral, and

---

[2] In Isaiah 61:9, one of the prophetic servant passages emphasizing the coming fulfillment of God's promises (see the discussion in chapter 4), the prophet used the same Hebrew word for "offspring" that is found in Genesis 12:7. As in Genesis, the form in Isaiah is a singular noun.

unholy, he did not inherit his father's blessing (cf. Gen 25:29-34; 27:1-40; Heb 12:16-17).

Jacob was not without fault either, deceiving both his brother and father to gain privileges that should have been Esau's. But in spite of his deceit, God chose Jacob to be the one through whom the promise would continue. He became the father of twelve sons, who became the ancestors and namesakes for the twelve tribes (groups) of people that made up the nation of Israel.[3]

Genesis 37, 39-50 tell the story of Jacob's eleventh son, Joseph. His ten older brothers were jealous of how Jacob favored him and sold him as a slave. The slave traders to whom they sold him took him to Egypt where he was sold again to Potiphar, the captain of Pharaoh's guard (37:12-35). After Potiphar's wife falsely accused him of making sexual advances toward her, Joseph was imprisoned (39:1-23). Later, because God blessed him with the ability to do so, he interpreted Pharaoh's obscure dream about seven years of bountiful crops followed by seven years of famine. Pharaoh then released him and made him the second most powerful man in Egypt (Gen 37:12-36; 39:1; 41:1-50).

After his trials, Joseph understood that God had been with him throughout all of them and was working to place him

---

[3] Jacob's twelve sons (and daughter Dinah) were born to his two wives, Leah and Rachel, and their two servants, Zilpah and Bilhah. In birth order, the sons were Reuben, Simeon, Levi, Judah, Dan, Naphtali, Gad, Asher, Issachar, Zebulun, Joseph, and Benjamin (cf. Gen 29-30; 35:18).

Allotments of territory in the land were given to descendants of all the sons except Levi. His descendants were designated to care for the tabernacle (later the temple) and its furnishings and services (cf. Num 1:48-54). The descendants of one levitical family (Aaron) were appointed to serve as the nation's priests. When giving his final blessings to his sons, Jacob claimed Manasseh and Ephraim, Joseph's sons, as his own and pronounced blessings on them (Gen 48:1-22). That action effectively elevated Manasseh and Ephraim to equal status with Joseph's brothers. In the land, allotments were designated for Ephraim and Manasseh (sometimes referred to as half-tribes; cf. Num 32:33), but not Joseph. Since Levi received no allotment (see Num 35:1-8), the number of territories remained at twelve.

in the position to rescue Jacob, his brothers, and their families from the famine about which Pharaoh had dreamed (Gen 50:20). The family left Canaan and went to Egypt, settling in the region of Goshen, one of the richest parts of the nation. They were put in charge of Pharaoh's livestock (Gen 47:1-7) and in time "gained possessions . . . and were fruitful and multiplied greatly" (v. 27).

3. Egyptian Slavery
Exodus 1-11 (ca. 1880-1450 BC)

Many years passed between the death of Joseph (Gen 50:22-26) and the events that led to Israel leaving Egypt. During that time, Jacob's family of seventy became "the people of Israel" who "multiplied and grew exceedingly strong, so that the land was filled with them" (Exod 1:7; cf. vv. 1-6; Gen 46:27). At an unspecified time during the period, a different ruling dynasty came to power in Egypt. The Bible says there was "a new king . . . who did not know Joseph" (Exod 1:8). That king, also known by the title Pharaoh, felt threatened by the increasing numbers of the Israelites in Goshen in the northeastern corner of the country. He was afraid that, if an enemy decided to attack Egypt from that direction, the Israelites would join the invaders and the combined force would overcome Egypt. Because of his fear, he enslaved the Israelites and forced them to serve under ruthless taskmasters who compelled them to build the store cities of Pithom and Raamses (Exod 1:9-11).

Israel's situation seemed hopeless. Although the people longed for their freedom, the Egyptians were too strong to overthrow. But, while God had told Abraham that his descendants would be servants in another land, he also promised that the time of their affliction would end (Gen 15:13). He sent Moses to deliver the Israelites from their slavery and lead them to the promised land.

As ancient peoples typically did, the Egyptians believed in multiple gods. Many believed that Pharaoh was in some sense divine. To prove he was superior to the Egyptian gods, the Lord, whom the Israelites would know as *Yahweh* (see Exod 3:13-16), afflicted Egypt with ten plagues, each of which showed God's superiority over something the Egyptians associated with one of their gods (Exod 7:14-12:32; cf. Num 33:4). The tenth plague brought death to the firstborn in every house not protected by God, including Pharaoh's. Scripture describes this event as follows:

> 29 At midnight the LORD struck down all the firstborn in the land of Egypt, from the firstborn of Pharaoh who sat on his throne to the firstborn of the captive who was in the dungeon, and all the firstborn of the livestock. 30 Pharaoh rose up in the night, he and all his servants and all the Egyptians. And there was a great cry in Egypt, for there was not a house where someone was not dead. 31 Then he summoned Moses and Aaron by night and said, "Up, go out from among my people, both you and the people of Israel; and go, serve the LORD, as you have said. 32 Take your flocks and your herds, as you have said, and be gone, and bless me also!" (Exod 12:29-32).

Israel's houses were spared from the wave of death that spread throughout Egypt in the tenth plague because they obeyed God. They put blood on their doorposts and lintels (a crossbeam at the top of the door). They also made the preparations he commanded for the meal they ate that night. From that time onward, Israel was to observe the Passover and Feast of Unleavened Bread to remember how God had delivered them from Egypt (cf. Exod 12:1-13:3).

4. Wilderness Wanderings
Exodus 12 - Deuteronomy 34 (ca. 1450-1410 BC)

After 430 years, the people of Israel left Egypt (Exod 12:40). Once they were freed from their slavery by the grace of God, the Israelites left Egypt and started for the promised land.

Their first test came soon after they left. Pharaoh and his servants decided they did not want to lose such a large group of laborers and pursued the Israelites to force them to return. Israel had camped by the Red Sea (Exod 14:2) and thought they were trapped between the pursuing Egyptian army and the water. The people cried out to the Lord and accused Moses of leading them into the wilderness to die. Once again, however, God's grace and power were revealed. He told Moses to tell the nation to move forward, divided the sea, and held back the waters as the Israelites crossed on dry ground. Then God allowed the waters to close in and destroy the Egyptian army as it attempted to follow the Israelites through the sea. Israel was finally free from both slavery and their fear of Pharaoh. They could move on toward Canaan (cf. Exod 14:1-31).

Three months after leaving Egypt, they arrived at Mount Sinai where God reminded them how he had chosen and delivered them. He then gave them the stipulations of his covenant, beginning with the Ten Commandments (Exod 19:1-20:21). Israel remained at Sinai while God gave Moses the details of the Law (Exod 20:22-Lev 27:34). Before they moved on, Moses took a census of the nation and they observed the Passover for the first time after leaving Egypt (Num 1:1-46; 9:4-5). They left Sinai and continued their journey "in the second year, in the second month, on the twentieth day of the month" after leaving Egypt (Num 10:11).

Israel had promised to do "all that the LORD has spoken" (Exod 19:8), but they continually complained about their difficulties in the wilderness (Num 11:1) and resisted Moses' leadership (cf. Deut 1:9-46). Because of their lack of faith, they forfeited their first opportunity to enter the promised land.

We read the details of this failure in Numbers 13-14. As they drew closer to the land, God told Moses to send twelve men, a leader from each tribe, "to spy out the land of Canaan" (Num 13:2). All twelve spies were in awe of the richness of the land and strength of its people, but ten of them were so overwhelmed by what they saw that they convinced the people they could not possibly defeat the Canaanites. Caleb and Joshua declared their faith that God would lead them to succeed and tried to convince Israel to move on. The pessimism of the other ten spies prevailed, however, and the people refused to advance.

Because of their lack of faith, God told them that all who were twenty years old or older would die in the wilderness and never enter Canaan. The only exceptions were Caleb and Joshua, the two faithful spies. It would be forty years after the Israelites left Egypt before they were permitted to cross the Jordan River and enter Canaan, one year for each of the forty days the spies were in the land (Num 14:34).

5. Conquering Canaan
Joshua 1-24 (ca. 1410-1390 BC)

Because of his own failure to trust in God in the wilderness, Moses was also prohibited from entering Canaan. A water shortage led the Israelites to complain again and accuse Moses of leading them into the wilderness just so they could die. God told Moses to speak to a rock and enough water would come from it to supply the people and livestock. Instead of merely speaking to the rock, however, Moses struck it twice with his staff. Water did flow from it and the nation's thirst was satisfied. But because Moses had not believed in the Lord and did not uphold his holiness before the people, he was not permitted to enter the promised land (Num 20:2-12).

Joshua, one of the two faithful spies, became Moses' assistant during Israel's time in the wilderness (Num 27:12-23; Deut 1:38). When Moses died (Deut 34:1-8), Joshua succeeded him as the nation's leader (34:9). Under his leadership, God led them across the flooded Jordan River and into Canaan (Josh 3:1-17). They began to take control of the land, just as God had promised. Notable in their conquest was the fall of Jericho, an event that occurred after they marched around the walls a total of thirteen times in a week (Josh 6:1-27).

Just as they had done under Moses, the people of Israel disobeyed under Joshua's leadership. By the end of his life, Israel had established themselves enough to continue to live in the land, but they failed to completely remove the people who had been living there as God had commanded them to do. Those people would continue to resist Israel, and the idolatry they practiced would tempt the Israelites. Joshua anticipated the latter problem in his final address to the people. He urged them to choose whether they would serve the gods their fathers had served in other places or would serve the Lord (*Yahweh*). He declared, "But as for me and my house, we will serve the LORD" (Josh 24:15).

6. Judges in Israel
Judges 1 - 1 Samuel 8 (ca. 1390-1050 BC)

In the years following Joshua's death, the nation of Israel no longer had a single leader. Each of the twelve tribes settled in the part of the land Moses had assigned to them (Josh 14:1-5). But they were more like twelve separate nations than a united country. Each tribe went its own way. Sometimes, the tribes fought each other (cf. Judg 20-21). They lacked the unity needed to be a strong nation.

In truth, they were supposed to be united under the kingship of God. In political terms, they were a theocracy, a form of government in which God or officials guided by him rule. But they were consistently unfaithful to the covenant between them and God. Because they often guided themselves instead of listening to God, some of their actions were exceedingly evil (cf. Judg 19:1-30). The book of Judges emphasized that their problem resulted from the fact that they tried to rule their own lives. Twice the book says that, "In those days there was no king in Israel. *everyone did what was right in his own eyes*" (Judg 17:6; 21:25).

That was not just what some of the individual people did. Whole tribes also did what was right in their own eyes (cf. 18:1; 19:1). They joined the people around them in worshiping idols and behaved as their neighbors did. They were not a distinct people showing God's holiness to the peoples around them (cf. Exod 19:5-6). Instead, they were participating in the same unholy way of life that characterized those peoples.

The book of Judges is a series of episodes that show this problem at different times and in different parts of the land. The stories have in common a four-part cycle. First, the people practiced the *sin* of the people around them. Second, because of their sin, they became *slaves* to a foreign nation. God allowed them to be enslaved so they would repent and obey him again. Third, after a period of oppression, the people experienced *sorrow* for their unfaithfulness and cried out to God for deliverance. Fourth, God sent a leader to deliver them and bring them *salvation* from their oppressors.

The leaders God sent were the *judges* from whom the book receives its name. These men and women were not judicial officials who heard and decided court cases, the way we use the word "judge" now. Instead, they were "leaders," "deliverers," or "rescuers," all words that are better translations of the Hebrew word than "judge." We know this from the way Judges 2:16 describes their work: "Then the LORD raised up *judges* [leaders; NET], who *saved* [delivered; NET] them out of the hand of those who plundered them."

After they had been delivered from their oppressors, the people would live faithfully for awhile. But as the book of Judges shows, the cycle of sin, slavery, sorrow, and salvation was repeated often. Things continued that way into the time of Samuel, the last judge (1 Sam 1-8). Eventually, in yet another effort to be like the nations around them, the people asked for a human king to rule over them.

We will take up that part of the story in chapter 6.

Additional Note: Chronological Resources & Historical Divisions

As noted above, determining the date of the exodus is one of the major chronological problems of Old Testament study. Proponents of both the early and late views base their arguments on key passages of Scripture and interpretation of archaeological evidence.

The details of the arguments are beyond the scope of this book. It is helpful, however, to be aware that debates of this kind occur. It is also useful to know where to find out more about chronology and the arguments made for and against the different views.

The following resources will help you to begin your study and provide a basic understanding of the Old Testament's chronology.

Lane T. Dennis, ed. *The ESV Study Bible.* Wheaton, IL: Crossway Bibles, 2008. See especially the article, "The Date of the Exodus" (p. 33), and other relevant background articles, timelines, and maps.

Andrew E. Hill and John H. Walton. *A Survey of the Old Testament.* 3rd ed. Grand Rapids, MI: Zondervan, 2009, pp. 65-67, 105-108.

William H. Shea, "Chronology of the Old Testament." In David Noel Freedman, ed., *Eerdmans Dictionary of the Bible.* Grand Rapids, MI: William B. Eerdmans Publishing Company, 2000, pp. 244-248.

John H. Walton. *Chronological and Background Charts of the Old Testament.* rev. ed. Grand Rapids, MI: Zondervan, 1994.

Dates in the chart below are based on consultation of multiple sources and are presented to help the reader develop a basic understanding of the different time periods included in the Bible's story.

Divisions of Bible History

	Theme	Bible Text	Early Exodus	Late Exodus
1	Creation to Abraham	Genesis 1-11	??-ca. 2095 BC	??-ca. 1895 BC
2	Patriarchal Period	Genesis 12-45; Job	ca. 2095-1880 BC	ca. 1895-1680 BC
3	Egyptian Slavery	Genesis 46 - Exodus 11	ca. 1880-1450 BC	ca. 1680-1250 BC
4	Wilderness Wanderings	Exodus 12-Deuteronomy 34*	ca. 1450-1410 BC	ca. 1250-1210 BC
5	Conquering Canaan	Joshua 1-24	ca. 1410-1390 BC	ca. 1210-1190 BC
6	Judges in Israel	Judges 1 - 1 Samuel 8	ca. 1390-1050 BC	1190-1025 BC
7	United Kingdom	1 Samuel 9 - 1 Kings 11*	1050-930 BC	1025-930 BC
8	Divided Kingdom	1 Kings 12:1 - 2 Kings 18:12*	930-722 BC	
9	Judah Alone	2 Kings 18:13 - 25:7*	722-586 BC	
10	Babylonian Exile	2 Kings 25:8-21*	586-516 BC	
11	Restoration of the Jews	Ezra & Nehemiah*	516-400 BC	
12	Intertestamental Period	———	400-4 BC	
13	Ministry of Jesus	Matthew 1 - Acts 1	4 BC - 30 AD	
14	The Church in Action	Acts 2 - Revelation 22	30-100 AD	

The Poetry books (Psalms-Song of Solomon) and Prophets (Isaiah-Malachi) include material from various time periods throughout the history covered by the Old Testament. The content of 1-2 Chronicles, emphasizing the beginning and development of David's dynasty, overlaps with part of the history as it is recorded in 1 Samuel through 2 Kings.

For Review and Thought

1. Explain the differences between ancient and modern dating and why we can be confident about when ancient events occurred.
2. What is the relationship of Genesis 1-11 to the rest of the Bible?
3. What do we learn about God in Genesis 1-2? In what ways does Genesis 1-2 show the special place of humanity in creation?
4. Define "sovereignty" as used in this chapter.
5. Based on the chapter's discussion of Genesis 2-3, explain the origin of human freedom and the relationship between freedom and consequences.
6. What three consequences resulted from the choice to eat the fruit God had forbidden?
7. How wicked was humanity by the time of Noah?
8. What were the three promises made to Abraham in Genesis 12?
9. In Galatians 3 and 4, Paul explained how the promises made to Abraham were fulfilled in Christianity. Explain what he said.
10. How long did Abraham wait between the time God called him and when Isaac was born? What Bible passages show this?
11. Beginning with Abraham, trace the promise through the Patriarchal Period from Abraham to the twelve tribes of Israel by giving the names of the individuals through whom the promise was passed on.
12. Summarize the story of Joseph from Genesis 37-50.
13. Who did God send to deliver Israel from Egypt?
14. What was the significance of the ten plagues? Why was the outcome of the tenth plague different for Egypt and Israel?
15. How was Israel finally freed from the control of Pharaoh? What did God tell Israel to do to remember how he delivered them?
16. Why did Israel stop for several months at Mount Sinai?
17. Why did the first generation that left Egypt not enter the land? Who were the exceptions? Why was Moses not allowed to enter?
18. Of what did Joshua warn Israel before he died? Did Israel listen? What were the consequences?
19. What Bible passages show how the people decided what was right during the judges period?
20. Identify and summarize the four parts of the cycle that was repeated throughout Judges.

CHAPTER 6

Kingdom: Successes and Setbacks

THE BOOK OF JUDGES ends by repeating a statement made previously regarding Israel's trust in themselves instead of God during the Judges Period. "In those days there was no king in Israel. Everyone did what was right in his own eyes" (Judg 21:25; cf. 17:6).

This verse informs us that conditions were not bad in Israel because they had no ruler, but because they did not submit to God as their ruler. It emphasizes that in the time of the judges, Israel had no earthly king. The wording of this verse anticipates that would change. Whoever recorded these words did so from the vantage point of a later time in which there was a king.

In addition to these observations, we should notice that the word "everyone" in Judges 21:25 is a generalization about the behavior of the people in Israel at that time. There were exceptions, people who followed God's law, not their own ways. The book of Ruth and 1 Samuel 1-8, also set in the Judges Period, show this. Those twelve chapters report the story of Ruth, Naomi, and Boaz, people who honored God with righteous lives (Ruth 1-4). They also tell about the last two judges in Israel, Eli and Samuel (1 Sam 1-8). Like the deliverers named in the book of Judges, both men demonstrated more trust in God than was typical in Israel generally.

Together, the stories of Ruth and Samuel set the stage for the beginning of the kingdom in Israel. Samuel anointed Israel's first two kings (1 Sam 9:16; 16:13). Ruth was the great-grandmother of David, Israel's greatest king (Ruth 4:17). In this chapter, we will survey the story of Israel after the appointment of an earthly king.

7. The United Kingdom
1 Samuel 9 - 1 Kings 11 (1050-930 BC)

The anointing of a king in Israel was itself evidence of the nation's unfaithfulness. Eli, who served as both priest and judge (1 Sam 1:9; 2:11; 4:18), had two sons whom he appointed as judges. But they were more interested in wealth than righteousness. In their role as priests, they took for themselves what was supposed to be devoted to God (2:11-17). In their role as judges, they took bribes and perverted justice (8:1-3).

Samuel, whom Eli raised in the house of God, was righteous (1:11, 27-28; 2:18-3:21), but the character of his sons was more like Eli's sons than their father (8:4). As Samuel reached old age, the elders of the people had taken note of the corruption of his sons and asked Samuel to appoint a king for them. Their concern about Samuel's sons was understandable, but the reason they gave when they asked for a king was so they would be "like all the nations" (8:5). Their request displeased Samuel, but God overrode his objection and told him to anoint a king as the people had asked. At the same time, God made it clear that the people's request was a rejection of his rule as king over them. He warned them that having a king would have adverse consequences (8:7-18).

Samuel anointed Saul, a man from the tribe of Benjamin, as the first king. At first, Saul was humble and so overwhelmed by the prospect of becoming king that he hid (1 Sam 9-10). However, he later took it upon himself to act on his own in disobedience to God's instructions. Through Samuel, God revealed to Saul that, because of his disobedience, his heirs would not be allowed to succeed him as king (1 Sam 13:13-14). Saul ruled for forty years (Acts 13:21).

After he told Saul that the kingdom would be taken from his house, Samuel anointed David, from the tribe of Judah, to be Saul's successor (1 Sam 16:13). After Saul's death, David reigned over Judah and Ish-bosheth, one of Saul's sons, ruled the rest of the kingdom (2 Sam 2:1-11). After war between the two factions, Ish-bosheth was assassinated and David became king of the entire nation (2 Sam 2-4). David was not sinless, but he was "a man after [God's] heart" (Acts 13:22; cf. 1 Sam 16:7). He generally proved to be a good ruler and Israel grew stronger during his reign. God promised that his heirs would succeed him and that his throne would be established forever (2 Sam 7:12-16). The coming of the Messiah was expected to be the ultimate fulfillment of this promise, something the New Testament writers showed they understood by emphasizing that Jesus was the son of David (cf. Acts 2:22-36; Heb 1:5; Matt 20:29-34).

Including his reigns over Judah alone and then Israel as a whole, David reigned forty years (2 Sam 5:4; 1 Kings 2:11). He defeated surrounding nations who had threatened and at times oppressed Israel since the time of the judges, most notably the Philistines, and began to enlarge Israel's borders. He was succeeded by Solomon, who also reigned forty years (1 Kings 11:42). Solomon was known for his wisdom, building the temple in Jerusalem, and great wealth (1 Kings 3:1-15; 4:29; 6:1-38; 10:23). Israel's broad influence continued during his reign (cf. 1 Kings 10:1-15). But Solomon also married 700 wives and had 300 concubines (1 Kings 11:3). Many of his marriages were arranged to secure political alliances, and as time went on "his wives turned away his heart after other gods, and his heart was not wholly true to the LORD his God, as was the heart of David his father" (v. 4). In what became the measurement for determining whether later kings were good or evil, the Bible says that "Solomon did what was evil in the sight of the LORD and did not wholly follow the LORD, as David his father had done" (v. 6). Therefore, "the LORD was angry with Solomon, because his heart had turned away from the LORD" (v. 9) to follow other gods. God told him that after his death, the majority of the kingdom would be taken from his son (vv. 10-13).

8. Divided Kingdom (Israel/Judah)
1 Kings 12 - 2 Kings 18:12 (930-722 BC)

Solomon's successor was his son, Rehoboam. At the beginning of his reign, the assembly of Israel approached him. Their leader was Jeroboam, a man who had returned from Egypt where he had fled to escape when Solomon tried to kill him because he "lifted up his hand against the king" (1 Kings 11:26-40). On behalf of the people, Jeroboam asked Rehoboam to lighten the burdens Solomon had imposed on the nation. Because he rejected the wisdom of his older advisers in favor of the counsel of younger men, Rehoboam responded that not only would he continue his father's policies, he would increase the burdens the people endured. When they heard this, ten of Israel's twelve tribes seceded from the kingdom and named Jeroboam their king. Only the tribes of Judah and Benjamin remained under Rehoboam's rule (1 Kings 12:1-21). The Israelites had become two nations. The ten tribes in the north part of the country were known as Israel. The remaining two tribes, in the south, were known as Judah.

Before fleeing to Egypt to escape Solomon, Jeroboam had been promised that if he would walk in God's ways and keep his commandments as David had done, the Lord would be with him and build him a strong house just as he built one for David (1 Kings 11:38). But Jeroboam feared that if the people of Israel returned to Jerusalem to worship in the temple, they would want to reunite with Judah and would kill him. Motivated by his fear, Jeroboam made two calves of gold and established new centers of worship for Israel in Bethel and Dan. He led Israel to embrace idolatry (12:25-33).

In all, Israel had twenty kings,[1] including a second man named Jeroboam (2 Kings 14:23-29). The kings came from nine different families or dynasties. Not one was a descendant of David and none followed his way of righteousness. Not all were said to be as wicked as Ahab who, encouraged by his queen Jezebel, "did more evil in sight of the LORD than all who were before him" (1 Kings 16:30; NET). But all of Israel's kings embraced idolatry and were declared to be evil in the accounts of their reigns found in 1-2 Kings (cf. 1 Kings 13:33; 2 Kings 15:18, 24, 28). They persecuted the prophets whom God sent to plead with Israel to turn away from idolatry, an appeal that ultimately failed (cf. 1 Kings 18-19; 22:8-28; Amos 7:11-17). Because of their idolatry and corresponding increase in wickedness, in 722 BC God permitted the empire of Assyria to conquer Samaria, Israel's capital. Hoshea was Israel's last king (2 Kings 17:6).

Second Kings 18:9-12 summarizes the last years of Israel as a nation and the reason it fell.

9 In the fourth year of King Hezekiah, which was the seventh year of Hoshea son of Elah, king of Israel, Shalmaneser king of Assyria came up against Samaria and besieged it, 10 and at the end of three years he took it. In the sixth year of Hezekiah, which was the ninth year of Hoshea king of Israel, Samaria was taken. 11 The king of Assyria carried the Israelites away to Assyria and put them in Halah, and on the Habor, the river of Gozan, and in the cities of the Medes, 12 because they did not obey the voice of the LORD their God but transgressed his covenant, even all that Moses the servant of the LORD commanded. They neither listened nor obeyed.

---

[1] This includes Tibni whom one faction of Israel accepted as king following the death of Zimri. The rival faction that favored Omri overcame the Tibni faction and Omri ruled as king over the entire nation (1 Kings 16:21-23).

9. Judah Alone
2 Kings 18:13-25:7 (722-586 BC)

Following Israel's destruction, Judah continued as a nation for about another 140 years. In their history as a separate nation, they were ruled by nineteen kings and a queen (Athaliah; 2 Kings 11:1-16). All of the kings were descendants of King David, but only eight of them "did what was right in the sight of the LORD," and only two of them, Hezekiah and Josiah, completely removed the idols that the people of Judah had erected (cf. 1 Kings 15:11, 14; 22:43; 2 Kings 12:2-3; 14:3-4; 15:3-4, 34-35; 18:3-5; 22:2, 11-13; 23:4-27).

The other eleven embraced idolatry and did evil just as the kings in Israel had done (cf. 2 Kings 11:1-3; 21:2, 19-20). Their unfaithfulness led Judah to suffer the same fate as Israel. By the early sixth century BC, Babylon had conquered Assyria and stood as the world's most powerful nation. Just as God had allowed Assyria to conquer Israel, he allowed Babylon to overthrow Judah. The nation's destruction was completed when the capital city of Jerusalem was destroyed in 586 BC (2 Kings 25:1-7). The Babylonians destroyed the temple, and except for some of the poorest people whom they left in the land to serve as vinedressers and plowmen, exiled the people of Judah to Babylon (25:8-21).

10. Babylonian Exile
2 Kings 25:8-21 (586-516 BC)

Like their ancestors whom Moses led out of Egypt, the Israelites were enslaved in Babylon. The prophet Jeremiah, who had foretold their fall, wrote a letter to the exiles with instructions about how they were to live in the foreign land. He told them to build houses and plant gardens, give their sons and daughters in marriage to one another, and seek the best interests of the cities in which they lived. He also told them not to expect the short exile that the false prophets among them were predicting (Jer 29:1-9).

Jeremiah predicted the people would live in exile for seventy years. God promised that, at the end of that time, they would be restored to their homeland. He said that, in spite of appearances, they had "a future and a hope" (Jer 29:9). When the time of exile was complete, they would call on the Lord and he would hear them. Unlike their ancestors who had repeatedly turned away from God, Jeremiah said that Israel would seek and find the Lord because they would seek him with all their hearts. He also said that God would restore their fortunes (Jer 29:10-14).

Near the end of the predicted time period, the prophet Daniel read Jeremiah's prediction that the exile would last seventy years and called on God to deliver them as he had promised (Dan 9:1-19).

11. Restoration of the Jews
Ezra & Nehemiah (516-400 BC)

By the end of the exilic period, Babylon had been conquered by the empire of the Medes and Persians. It was the Persians who allowed God's people to return to their land. When they did so, they had to rebuild the city of Jerusalem and the temple. They also had to be taught God's law. They faced opposition to their rebuilding efforts from other peoples who had been living in the land while they were away. Their enemies taunted them, sent negative reports about them to the Persians, and worked against them to keep the walls of Jerusalem from being rebuilt (cf. Ezra 4:7-24; Neh 4:1-3; 6:1-9).

Ezra, a scribe, and Nehemiah, who had been a cupbearer in the court of the Persian king Artaxerxes, led the rebuilding of both the walls of Jerusalem and the spiritual strength of the people. Ezra focused on teaching the people the law and how to honor it. Nehemiah was granted a commission from

Artaxerxes to take charge of rebuilding Jerusalem's walls (see the books of Ezra and Nehemiah).

The people did not always follow God perfectly after returning to the land. The prophet Haggai rebuked them for building their own houses before they finished the temple, God's house (Hag 1-2). Later, Malachi rebuked them for offering blemished sacrifices to God and for the corruption of the priesthood (Mal 1-2). But the people did not resume the idolatrous ways that had characterized their ancestors and led to the nation's fall.

They knew, however, that they were not as strong and influential as they had been in the glorious days of David. They also knew that God had promised that a time would come when he would send a king like David and would restore their fortunes. As the Old Testament concluded with the book of Malachi, it ended with a message of hope about that future time. Two passages are noteworthy.

> 1 Behold, I send my messenger, and he will prepare the way before me. And the Lord whom you seek will suddenly come to his temple; and the messenger of the covenant in whom you delight, behold, he is coming, says the LORD of hosts. 2 But who can endure the day of his coming, and who can stand when he appears? For he is like a refiner's fire and like fullers' soap. 3 He will sit as a refiner and purifier of silver, and he will purify the sons of Levi and refine them like gold and silver, and they will bring offerings in righteousness to the LORD. 4 Then the offering of Judah and Jerusalem will be pleasing to the LORD as in the days of old and as in former years (Mal 3:1-4).

> 5 Behold, I will send you Elijah the prophet before the great and awesome day of the LORD comes. 6 And he will turn the hearts of fathers to their children and the hearts of children to their fathers, lest I come and strike the land with a decree of utter destruction (Mal 4:5-6).

Additional Note: Kings of Judah and Israel

Judah		Israel	
King	1st Reference	King	1st Reference
Rehoboam	1 Kings 12:1	Jeroboam I	1 Kings 12:20
Abijah/Abijam	1 Kings 15:1	Nadab	1 Kings 15:25
Asa	1 Kings 15:9	Baashaa	1 Kings 15:27
Jehoshaphat	1 Kings 22:41	Elah	1 Kings 16:8
Jehoram/Joram	2 Kings 8:16	Zimri	1 Kings 16:10
Ahaziah	2 Kings 8:25	Tibni vs. Omri	1 Kings 16:21-23
Athaliah (Q)	2 Kings 11:1-3	Omri	1 Kings 16:16
Joash/Jehoash	2 Kings 12:1	Ahab	1 Kings 16:29
Amaziah	2 Kings 14:1	Ahaziah	1 Kings 22:51
Uzziah/Azariah	2 Kings 15:1	Joram/Jehoram	2 Kings 3:1
Jotham	2 Kings 15:32	Jehu	2 Kings 9:8
Ahaz	2 Kings 16:1	Jehoahaz	2 Kings 13:1-9
Hezekiah	2 Kings 18:1	Joash/Jehoash	2 Kings 13:1
Manasseh	2 Kings 21:1	Jeroboam II	2 Kings 14:23
Amon	2 Kings 21:19	Zechariah	2 Kings 15:8
Josiah	2 Kings 22:1	Shallum	2 Kings 15:10
Jehoahaz	2 Kings 23:31	Menahem	2 Kings 15:14
Jehoiakim	2 Kings 23:36	Pekahiah	2 Kings 15:23
Jehoiachin/Jeconiah	2 Kings 24:8	Pekah	2 Kings 15:25
Zedekiah	2 Kings 24:18	Hoshea	2 Kings 15:30

- *Passages listed are references that announce the beginning of each ruler's reign.*
- *Judah kings in* **bold** *type are those the Bible says "did what was right in the eyes of the LORD."*
- *The names of Hezekiah and Josiah are in* **bold italics** *because they went beyond what the other good kings did and removed the idols the people had erected.*
- *Kings for whom two names are given were referred to in Scripture by both names.*

For Review and Thought

1. "Everyone did what was right in his own eyes" (Judg 17:6; 21:25). What shows that this statement is a generalization?

2. What was the relationship of Samuel and Ruth to the first kings of Israel?

3. Why did the elders of Israel ask Samuel for a king? How did Samuel react?

4. Who was Israel's first king? How long did he reign? Why were his heirs not allowed to succeed him?

5. Who was the second king Samuel anointed? How long did he reign? What promises did God make about his heirs? Who succeeded him?

6. For what accomplishments and mistakes is King Solomon known? According to 1 Kings 11:6, what was his legacy? Why is this important in Israel's history?

7. Who succeeded Solomon and what mistake did he make at the beginning of his reign? What were the consequences?

8. Who led the rebellion against Rehoboam and began a new kingdom? What were the two kingdoms called? What tribes remained with Rehoboam?

9. Why did Jeroboam establish new worship centers in Bethel and Dan? What was the result?

10. Who did God send to try to convince Israel to return to him? What empire destroyed Samaria, Israel's capital city? When did this occur? What happened to most of the people?

11. Compare Judah's record of faithfulness to God to Israel's record. Who destroyed Jerusalem, Judah's capital city? When did this occur? What happened to many of the people?

12. How long did Jeremiah tell the people the exile would last? What did he tell the exiles to do while they were in Babylon?

13. Who conquered Babylon and allowed the exiles to return home? What two obstacles did they have to overcome when they returned? Who led them in overcoming these problems?

14. For what did Haggai and Malachi rebuke the people after they returned to Israel?

15. With what message of hope does the Old Testament end? Why was this assurance important to Israel?

CHAPTER 7

"The Fullness of Time"

12. Intertestamental Period (400 - 4 BC)

SINCE NONE OF THE Bible's books come from the era, some might feel justified in by-passing the twelfth historical period and moving on to the New Testament. You could, therefore, elect to skip this chapter and continue your study of the Bible's story in chapter 8.

But before you do, think for a moment how it would affect our understanding of our world if, in a United States history course, we studied the planting of the colonies in Jamestown (1607) and Plymouth Rock (1620) and then skipped everything between the 1620s and the 1960s. Or, for a better parallel since the lengths of time for the complete stories are comparable, think about how it would affect our understanding of Western civilization if we studied the events from the time of the Roman empire until the early 1600s and then skipped to the 1960s. The point is, our understanding of the world will be sorely lacking if we are not at least somewhat knowledgeable of the events of the last four centuries.

The same is true when it comes to understanding the New Testament era where the events begin 400 years after the close of the Old. Considering it first in terms of world history, at the end of the Old Testament, the ruling power was Persia, but in the time of the New Testament, the dominant empire was Rome. Between the times of the Persian and Roman reigns, a Greek empire, first united and then divided, ruled and the Jews experienced a period of independence.

We face the same issue when we narrow our focus to consider the Bible's story. The Old Testament was written in Hebrew, but the New Testament was written in Greek. Why is that? In the Old Testament, we read nothing about synagogues, Pharisees, or Sadducees, but all figure prominently in the ministry of Jesus and experiences of the earliest churches. These examples illustrate how our understanding of the New Testament will be more complete if we know about the events that occurred during the 400 years between the testaments.

A comment by the apostle Paul about the coming of God's Son into the world reveals another reason for learning about the time between the Testaments. In Galatians 3 and 4, he recalled the promises made to Abraham in Genesis 12 and explained the relationship of the Law of Moses to those promises. He emphasized that the goal of God's plan was to save all people through the work of his Son. In that context, he said, "But when the fullness of time had come, God sent forth his Son, born of a woman, born under the law" (Gal 4:4). The New English Translation (NET) says, "But when *the appropriate time* had come, God sent out his Son, born of a woman, born under the law." What about the time of Jesus' coming made it "the appropriate time"? Knowledge of events in the Intertestamental Period helps us answer that question. At the same time, we gain greater appreciation for how God worked in the world to complete his plan.

The Persian Period (535-331 BC)

As we saw in chapter 6, during the time God's people were exiled from their land, the Persians conquered the Babylonians and became the dominant world empire (539 BC). The exile made it necessary for the Israelites to re-think how they were to approach God and learn about his ways. The Babylonians destroyed the temple, removing what had been the focal point of their worship to God. As a scattered people, they needed a place where they could teach, pray, worship, and gather as a community. Although we have no specific information about the origin of the synagogue, we do know that it met all of these needs. We also know that synagogues were present in nearly all Palestinian cities and towns and throughout the Mediterranean world. This indicates that they existed during the Intertestamental Period and probably originated during the exile.

Cyrus, a Persian ruler, granted permission to the exiles to return to their land and rebuild the temple in Jerusalem. He decreed that those who returned would be assisted by their neighbors who were to supply the Jews with what they needed for the temple and its worship. This included silver and gold, equipment, animals, and voluntary offerings for the temple (Ezra 1:1-4).

Not all the Jews chose to return, however. Some who did not were later deported to other parts of the world to help the empire establish stability in other places. The scattering, or dispersion that resulted, is known by its Greek term, *Diaspora*. It was significant for the spread of Christianity "in the fullness of time" (Gal 4:4). Because of the *Diaspora*, Jewish communities, most of which had synagogues, were scattered throughout the Greco-Roman world. As a result, many non-Jewish people became familiar with, and in some cases were attracted to, the core teachings of Judaism, particularly monotheism. This gave the Christian missionaries who took the gospel into those communities a place to begin their teaching, a ready-made audience of people who were knowledgeable of the Jewish teachings from which the Christian faith developed.

The Persians also contributed to the fullness of time in other ways. The government established order throughout the world that was unlike what had been known before. Later empires copied and adapted features of the Persian methods, especially their attention to law and order. These standards made conditions in the world more stable, a circumstance that would facilitate the spread of Christianity.

Greek (Hellenistic) Period (331-167 BC)

Just as the Persians had conquered the Babylonians, the Greeks conquered the Persians. The history of the Greek, or Hellenistic,[1] empire is divided into two periods, united and divided.

Alexander the Great is more popularly known, but the Greek empire began its rise to prominence under his father, Philip II of Macedon. By 338 BC, Philip, an ambitious ruler, had consolidated the rival factions of a confederation of Greek city-states into a united rule. He believed that Greek forms of art, literature, and architecture were superior to all others and was determined to spread the Greek way of life. He set out to overthrow the Persians, but died in 336 BC before realizing his goal.

At the age of 19, Alexander succeeded his father and proved himself capable of leading the growing empire. By 331 BC, he had defeated the Persians in battle at Grannicus and Issus, liberated Egypt from Persian rule, and conquered Darius III in the battle of Guagamela. After conquering the Persians, he continued to advance to the east, eventually extending the Greek empire to northern India. He accomplished all this in just thirteen years after his father's death. He died in Babylon in 323 BC.

The most notable accomplishment in Alexander's legacy is that he brought together the East and West and spread Greek culture from Europe to India. He spread the Greek spirit of individual liberty, stirring a desire for freedom from custom and tradition. He encouraged the free exercise of science and critical inquiry. He spread a love for the beautiful in art and literature and encouraged people throughout the entire empire to develop their minds and bodies. He sought to break down

---

[1] "Hellenistic" is derived from the Greek word *Hellas*, the original word for Greece.

racial and national barriers and initiated a spirit of cosmopolitanism. Most significantly, he spread the Greek language which became the common language across the ancient world.

After Alexander's death, a struggle for control of his empire was settled when it was divided among his four generals. The areas controlled by two of them are most relevant for understanding events in Israel. Syria, which was centered in the area just north of Judea, was controlled by Seleucus and his descendants, the Seleucids. Egypt was the center of the region ruled by Ptolemy and his descendants, the Ptolemies.

Located geographically between them, Judea was caught in the power struggle between the competing Greek powers. The land's strategic location at the crossroads of important trade routes between Africa, Asia, and Europe made it a natural territorial buffer. Its location also made Judea vulnerable to invasion by powers who sought control for military and economic purposes. In addition, both the Seleucids and Ptolemies coveted its natural resources and tax revenue.

At first, the Ptolemies controlled the land (301-198 BC). This was a relatively peaceful time for Judea. It was also a time when the lines between Greek and Jewish culture outside Judea began to blur. It was in a Jewish colony in Alexandria, Egypt that a translation of the Hebrew Scriptures into Greek was completed from about 285-257 BC. Because of a tradition that seventy translators produced it, the translation is called the Septuagint (abbreviated LXX, the Roman numeral for 70). It was the principal Greek Bible of first century AD Jews and Christians throughout the Greco-Roman world and is most often the translation used for Old Testament citations found in the New Testament.

At the beginning of the second century BC, the Seleucids (Syrians) pushed the Ptolemies out of Judea and ruled the region from 198-167 BC. This period, which began under the rule of Antiochus III the Great (223-187 BC), was not as peaceful for Judea as the years under the Ptolemies had been. Their troubles intensified during the reign of Antiochus IV Epiphanes[2] (175-164 BC), the son who succeeded Antiochus III. He was determined that the Jews would submit to the ideals of Greek culture as well as to Greek rule.

Through the use of both legislation and oppression, Antiochus set out to force the Jews to give up their unique practices and religion. In 168 BC, he attacked and devastated the city of Jerusalem. He ransacked the temple and defiled it by erecting a statue of the Greek god Zeus and offering sacrifices of animals such as pigs on the site of the altar. These acts were viewed as abominations by the Jews. He also prohibited temple worship and insisted that the Jews build shrines and offer sacrifices to Greek gods. Under penalty of death, he prohibited circumcision and set out to destroy all copies of the Jewish Scriptures. Finally, he compelled the people to publicly renounce their Jewish ways and profess loyalty to him as king.

Period of Independence (167-63 BC)

The pressure Antiochus exerted on the Jews led to a rebellion that began in Modein, a village not far from Jerusalem. To set an example for the villagers, Seleucid officers ordered a priest named Mattathias to offer a sacrifice to Greek deities and declare his loyalty to Antiochus. When Mattathias refused, another Jew stepped forward to obey the order and offer the sacrifice. An angry Mattathias killed the man and the Seleucid official and then destroyed the altar. He and his five sons then fled into the hill country where they were joined by other rebels and began to wage war against the Seleucids. Among those who joined them were the Hasideans, a group committed to the Law and to resisting the impositions of the Greeks.[3]

---

[2] "Epiphanes" was actually a title that meant, "the manifest one." Antiochus preferred it because of his belief that he possessed divine qualities.

[3] One account of the Greek persecution and the rebellion, told from the Jewish perspective, is found in chapter 2 of the intertestamental writing *1 Maccabees*, one of the books in the Apocrypha (see pp. 105-106).

When Mattathias died, leadership of the revolt passed to his son, Judas, called Maccabeus (the Hammer). Since he was the principal leader of the rebellion (166-160 BC), it is known as the Maccabean Revolt. Judas was a skilled military strategist who led the rebels to multiple victories over the superior Seleucid forces. He succeeded in liberating the temple in 164 BC and rededicated it to God in December of that year. To commemorate the rededication, the Feast of Dedication, known as Hanukkah or the Feast of Lights, was established (cf. John 10:22). Since the rebellion had won religious freedom from the Syrians, the Hasideans left the movement, refusing to follow Judas as he continued to seek political independence.[4]

After Judas was killed in battle, his brother Jonathan became the leader of the revolt (160-142 BC). In his effort to gain political independence from the Syrians, he made alliances with Rome and Sparta and began to combine secular rule with the office of the high priest.

When Jonathan was captured and killed by Trypho, another enemy of the Syrians, Simon, a third son of Mattathias, succeeded him (142-135 BC). It was under his leadership that the people achieved political independence. His reign was comparatively peaceful. He was a transitional figure, the last revolutionary Maccabean and the first of the more established Hasmonean dynasty who ruled after his death.

John Hyrcanus I (135-104 BC), Simon's son and successor, was the first Hasmonean ruler after Simon. Three notable developments that significantly impacted events in the New Testament era occurred during his reign. First, Hyrcanus conquered the Samaritans, destroyed their temple on Mount Gerizim,[5] and forced them to accept the Jewish religion. Second, the Idumeans, descendants of Esau and longtime enemies of Israel, were also Judaized. Third, the more important Jewish

---

[4] It was from within the Hasideans that the party of the Pharisees developed.

[5] Josephus mentions the origin and location of the Samaritan temple in his *Antiquities* 11.8.2 [§ 310]. For more on Josephus, see p. 107.

religio-political sects, or parties, notably the Pharisees and Sadducees, grew stronger.[6] The Pharisees were a small, strict, and respected party whose members were committed to being loyal to the Law and resisting foreign influences and practices that compromised Israel's purity. The Sadducees drew their members from the wealthy landowning class and the priesthood, although not all priests were Sadducees. They were politically active and accommodating to the influences of Greek culture. The groups also differed theologically, as Luke reported when he wrote, "The Sadducees say that there is no resurrection, or angel, or spirit; but the Pharisees acknowledge all three" (Acts 23:8).

After Hyrcanus died, Aristobulus I, his son, conquered Galilee. Succeeding rulers proved to be both less able and more wicked. Political schemes designed to either gain or retain power became the norm. Eventually, rule of the kingdom was passed down to two brothers, Hyrcanus II and Aristobulus II, who feuded over who would prevail.

The Roman Period (63 BC - 70 AD)[7]

The Jews lost their independence in 63 BC. The Roman general Pompey accepted the invitation of Hyrcanus II and Aristobulus II to mediate their dispute over who was the rightful ruler and used the opportunity to take control of Judea for the Romans. Antipater, the governor of Idumea, took advantage of the situation to secure favor with the Romans who appointed him to govern the region for them. He appointed his two sons to rule the main parts of Israel; Phaezael ruled Judea and Herod ruled Galilee. When Antipater died, Herod maneuvered his way into ruling the entire land, betraying friends like Marc Antony to gain control. He ruled all Israel for Rome as a client king, a

---

6 Josephus reports that the Pharisees, Sadducees, and a group known as the Essenes all had their origins during the time of Jonathan (*Antiquities* 13.5.9 [§ 171]).

7 Roman rule over Palestine did not end in 70 AD. The date is used here because 70 AD was when the Romans destroyed Jerusalem and the temple.

ruler who derived his authority from the superior Roman power and served the empire's interests over those of his subjects.

Herod's reign can be divided into three periods. From 37-28 BC, he consolidated his power. The middle period (28-14 BC) was devoted to building projects. Because of his Idumean heritage and the way he ruled, Herod was disliked by his Jewish subjects. He tried to appease them by an extensive building program. The centerpiece of his projects was an elaborate addition to the Second Temple that had been built in the time of Zerubbabel after the return from the Babylonian exile (see the Old Testament books of Ezra, Nehemiah, Haggai, and Zechariah).

The third period of Herod's reign (14-4 BC) was devoted to holding on to power. He became increasingly suspicious and consumed by jealous rage. He killed people he believed were threats to his power, including his favorite wife. In view of the extent of his wickedness during this period, the report that he ordered the murder of all the infant boys in and around Bethlehem in order to eliminate a future rival is eminently believable (see Matt 2:16-18).

After his death in 4 BC, Herod's kingdom was divided among three of his sons. Archelaus (4 BC - 6 AD) ruled Judea, Samaria, and Idumea. He was unable to establish stability, however, and was deposed by the Romans who replaced him with an appointed official known as a procurator.[8] Herod Antipas (4 BC - 39 AD) ruled as tetrarch over Galilee and Perea. During

---

[8] In 27 BC, the emperor Augustus divided the thirty-two Roman provinces into two categories, senatorial (11) and imperial (21). Senatorial provinces were regions that had long been under Roman control and were generally more peaceful and easier to rule. These provinces were governed by officials known as proconsuls, each of whom was appointed for a one-year term (see Acts 13:7-8, 12; 18:12).

Imperial provinces were territories that were newer additions to the empire, places where rulers had to contend with revolutionaries and civil strife. The emperor directly appointed the rulers of these areas, "legates" in the larger provinces, and "procurators" to govern the smaller provinces. The word "procurator" never appears in English translations which use "governor" instead (see Luke 3:1; 20:20; Acts 23:24-33; etc.).

his reign, he arrested and killed John the Baptist after John challenged the lawfulness of his marriage to Herodias who had been the wife of his half-brother (cf. Matt 14:1-12; Mark 6:17-29; Luke 3:19-20). That brother was Herod Philip (4 BC - 34 AD) who ruled as tetrarch of a region that included Iturea and Trachonitus. Because fewer Jews lived in that area, he faced less turmoil than the other rulers did. He built the city of Caesarea Philippi in honor of Caesar Augustus.

A fourth son of Herod the Great, Aristobulus, was the father of Herod Agrippa I who ruled a territory that was nearly as large as his grandfather's had been (AD 37-44). Under his rule, the Romans released Judea from the control of a procurator for a time. His son, Herod Agrippa II (48-70 AD), ruled as tetrarch over Chalcis and the northern territory. Paul appeared before him before being sent to Rome (Acts 26).

During the middle years of the first century AD, tensions that had long existed between the Jewish people and the Romans increased. One group, the Zealots, actively resisted Roman rule. More extreme dissidents advocated violent resistance and assassination (cf. Acts 21:38), adding to the growing unrest. Jewish leaders, including Herod Agrippa II, tried to mediate between the Romans and the revolutionaries, but fighting broke out in 66 AD. The subsequent war led to the destruction of Jerusalem and the temple by the Roman general Titus in 70 AD. The changes Judaism experienced from the loss of their capital and temple were comparable to what had occurred after the Babylonians destroyed Jerusalem in 586 BC. Many Jews perished during the war from 66-70. Thousands were enslaved or kept for Roman gladiatorial games, and only a remnant remained in Judea. The loss of the temple forced the Jews to rethink how to practice their religion, and the Jews of the *Diaspora* became more important than those who lived in the homeland.

Impact of the Intertestamental Period

This survey has merely introduced this fascinating period of history. Hopefully it is sufficient to show the importance of the web of ideas, choices, and activities that shaped the culture and events of the time of the New Testament. Study of the Intertestamental Period reminds us that the things reported in the Bible did not occur in a historical vacuum, or, as Paul said, "in a corner" (Acts 26:26). Bible events were part of the history of that time. They influenced and were influenced by other events of the period. To put it another way, people reacted to Jesus and his followers the way they did in light of the circumstances that had been created in the history of their society and world as a whole. It is important to at least generally understand the history of that time and place in order to more completely understand the sense in which God sent his Son "when the appropriate time came" (Gal 4:4; NET).

We will conclude this chapter with a review of the impact of the Greeks, Romans, and circumstances in Judea on Christianity's entrance into the world.

First, because of the conquest and missionary zeal of Alexander the Great and his successors, Greek culture, language, and education had a broad influence in the time of the New Testament, including in Judea. Greek was the international language of the ancient world, much like English is in today's world. The Old Testament Scriptures had been translated into Greek, an occurrence that made the story of God's plan through Israel accessible to a much larger audience than would have been the case had the Jewish Scriptures been available only in Hebrew.

By the late first century BC, the Romans had replaced the Greeks as the dominant power in the world. They did not replace Greek culture, but built on it. They improved law and order throughout the ancient world. In order to facilitate the movement of their armies across the empire, they built a system of good roads, some of which remain to the present. The

Romans' attention to these issues made travel easier for everyone, including Christian missionaries. More importantly, the Romans were so firmly in control that there was relatively little unrest in the world. A period of peace, called the Pax Romana (Roman Peace), left the people without the anxiety that accompanies turmoil and war. People were free to listen to new ideas like the good news the Christians were telling.

Conditions in Judea also contributed to "the fullness of time." The Jews remembered the promises about a coming Son of David who would restore the glory of his kingdom. They were anxious for his arrival, a longing made more acute by their forced submission to the Romans. Furthermore, their view of what his reign would be like led them to expect a different sort of king than Jesus would prove to be.

Politically, the forced annexation of Samaria, Idumea, and Galilee created tensions that hardened attitudes and biases, kept trouble brewing, and made Judea one of the most difficult places for the Romans to rule. The differing beliefs, practices, and agendas of parties such as the Pharisees, Sadducees, and Zealots added to the unrest. Their views and place in society also made it hard for them to hear Jesus' teaching. He often found himself caught between the parties and at odds with their various interpretations and traditions (cf. Mark 11:27-12:40).

Finally, the common people, oppressed by the Romans and either ignored or discounted by the powerful insiders in the different Jewish parties, longed for deliverance and for God to keep his promise to send the deliverer, his Messiah.

The four hundred years between the Testaments set the stage for his arrival and the completion of God's plan.

Additional Note 1: Primary Resources for Studying the Intertestamental Period

The preceding summary is sufficient for us to see that even though the Scriptures are silent about the events from 400-4 BC, many things occurred and ways of thinking were formulated that had a profound impact on conditions in the first century AD, the time of the New Testament. The following primary resources are particularly helpful for understanding first century AD Jewish culture in Palestine.

The Apocrypha

Apocrypha, a word that originally meant "hidden" or "obscure," refers to a group of Jewish books and supplements to Hebrew biblical texts. Some groups include the books as part of the canon, the official list of books considered to be Scripture.[9] But there is little evidence that Jews in Palestine accepted them as being equal in authority to the thirty-nine Old Testament writings. The dates of origin for the writings range from the late third century BC to the first century AD.

Most of the books were originally written in Greek, and the Septuagint (LXX) interspersed them among the thirty-nine Old Testament books. Eastern Orthodox believers and Roman Catholics considered them canonical, a position the Roman Church reaffirmed at the Council of Trent in the mid-16th century.[10] But Protestants such as Martin Luther and the Anglican

---

[9] "Canon" and "canonical" derive from the Greek word, *kanōn*, a rule or standard. As used here, it refers to the books that are accepted as authoritative Scripture.

[10] Currently, Romans Catholics use the term "Deuterocanonical," literally "second canon," to refer to these books. By this, they do not mean that the books have a secondary status, but that they became canonical at a later date, in contrast to the "Protocanonical," "first canon," Hebrew texts. The Eastern Church also uses "Deuterocanonical" to refer to the books, reserving the term "Apocrypha" to refer to other books more commonly known as "Pseudepigrapa" (see below).

It should also be noted that some refer to these books as the "Old Testament" or "Jewish" Apocrypha to distinguish them from a later collection of writings known as the "Christian" or "New Testament" Apocrypha.

Church accepted them only for private education. Consequently, believers in the Protestant tradition typically do not accept them as part of the Old Testament canon.

Although some collections include other writings, lists of the Apocrypha generally include fifteen books. They are written in various literary styles.

1. Historical: *1, 2 Maccabees, 1 Esdras* (also called *3 Ezra*).
2. Legends, novels, folktales, and detective stories: *Judith, Tobit,* and three additions to the Old Testament book of Daniel—*Susanna, Bel and the Dragon,* and the *Song of the Three Young Men.*
3. Wisdom or Didactic (intended to teach): *Baruch, Epistle of Jeremiah, Wisdom of Solomon, Ecclesiasticus* (also called the *Wisdom of Jesus Son of Sirach* or just *Sirach*).
4. Prayers or religious themes: *Prayer of Manasseh, Additions to Esther.*
5. Apocalyptic:[11] *2 Esdras* (also called *4 Ezra*).

The Pseudepigrapha

Pseudepigrapha refers to Jewish writings that were excluded from the Old Testament canon and are generally omitted from the Apocrypha (although there is some overlapping, depending on who compiles the respective lists). Although these writings were never considered part of the canon, they are valuable sources of information for understanding the content and development of Jewish thought during the Intertestamental Period. They also provide important background information about conditions in the time of the New Testament. They were written between 200 BC and 200 AD, and are divided into two groups, Palestinian writings and Jewish-Hellenistic (Greek) writings. They were written in one of three literary styles: poetry, legend, and apocalyptic.

---

[11] "Apocalyptic" is from a Greek word (*apokalupsis*) that meant "unveiling, revealing." Apocalyptic writings claim to unveil or reveal the future. Their authors used images and symbols to convey their messages. Writings in the apocalyptic style from the Old Testament and Intertestamental Period are valuable resources for understanding the images and symbols in the New Testament book of Revelation, sometimes called "The Apocalypse."

Although they were originally Jewish writings, there is evidence that some were edited by early Christian writers. Important themes in the books include attacks on idolatry, statements of increased reverence for the Law, arguments against the emphasis on the temple (for example, some of the books are anti-Sadducean writings of the Pharisees), and the expectation of fulfilled promises.

Most prominent among the pseudepigraphal writings are *Psalms of Solomon, Testaments of the Twelve Patriarchs, Jubilees, Testament of Job, 1-3 Enoch, Sibylline Oracles, The Assumption of Moses,* and *3-4 Maccabees.*

The Writings of Josephus

Josephus (ca. 37-100 AD) was a Jewish soldier and historian born in Jerusalem to a father who was a priest and a mother who claimed royal ancestry. He initially fought against the Romans in the First Jewish-Roman War (66-70 AD), but surrendered to the Roman general Vespasian. Favored by the general, Josephus became a Roman slave and interpreter who was granted his freedom when Vespasian became Emperor (69 AD). He defected to the Romans and was granted citizenship.

The writings of Josephus provide a record of Jewish history, especially the events of the first century AD and the Jewish-Roman War. His works include *Jewish Wars,* a record of the struggles of the Jews from 170 BC until the time of his writing in the late first century AD; *Antiquities of the Jews,* a history of the Jews from creation to the first century AD; an autobiography, called *Life,* in which he answered charges regarding his conduct in the Jewish War; and *Against Apion,* a defense of Judaism against detractors from the previous three centuries. Although his accounts are highly rhetorical, they provide valuable information about the environment in which Christianity began from someone who lived close enough to the events (the Maccabean revolt, for example) to be aware of important primary source information.

Additional Note 2: Secondary Resources

The following sources were helpful for preparing the summary and notes in this chapter.

David Noel Freedman, ed. *Eerdmans Dictionary of the Bible.* Grand Rapids, MI: William B. Eerdmans Publishing Company, 2000.

Bruce M. Metzger. *The New Testament: Its Background, Growth, and Content.* 3rd ed. Revised & Enlarged. Nashville, TN: Abingdon Press, 2003.

J. Julius Scott, Jr. "The Time Between the Testaments." In *ESV Study Bible.* ed. Lane T. Dennis. Wheaton, IL: Crossway Bibles, 2008, pp. 1783-1791.

Marsha A. Ellis Smith, ed. *Holman Book of Biblical Charts, Maps, and Reconstructions.* Nashville, TN: Broadman & Holman Publishers, 1993.

T. C. Smith. "The Religious and Cultural Background of the New Testament," in *The Broadman Bible Commentary*, vol. 8, General Articles, Matthew-Mark, ed. Clifton J. Allen. Nashville, TN: Broadman Press, 1971, pp. 1-14.

For a more elaborate, although still relatively brief (136 pages) and readable survey, see:

Charles F. Pfeiffer. *Between the Testaments.* Grand Rapids, MI: Baker Book House, 1959.

For Review and Thought

1. Explain why it is important to study the Intertestamental Period even though no Bible book came from that period.

2. Name some things that we read about in the New Testament that are not mentioned in the Old, but are referred to in writings from the Intertestamental Period.

3. What is the significance of Galatians 4:4 for a study of the Intertestamental Period?

4. What Jewish needs were addressed by the synagogue? What do we know about its origins and development?

5. Identify the *Diaspora* and explain its importance for Jews and Christians in the Intertestamental and early Christian periods.

6. Identify Philip II of Macedon and Alexander the Great. For "the fullness of time," what is most notable about Alexander's legacy?

7. Who succeeded Alexander? What ruling dynasties are relevant for events in Palestine?

8. When did the Ptolemies rule Palestine? What notable development occurred during the period that had a significant impact on Jews and Christians in the first century AD?

9. When did the Seleucids (Syrians) rule Palestine? What were conditions like during their reign?

10. Name some specific things Antiochus Epiphanes did as part of his effort to force the Jews to conform to Greek ways.

11. Describe the events and major parties involved in the Jewish rebellion against the Seleucids. What name was given to the revolt?

12. Name, give the dates of leadership, and briefly describe key events for the three leaders in the Maccabean Revolt.

13. Who succeeded Simon as ruler in the Hasmonean Period? When did he rule? What notable events occurred during his reign?

14. Describe notable rulers, events, and their consequences in the years after Hyrcanus I.

15. When did the Jews lose their independence? To whom (nation and general)? How did this come about?

16. Identify Antipater, Phazael, and Herod and describe events that led to the latter being appointed king of the Jews by the Romans.

17. Give the dates and briefly describe the key events in the three parts of Herod's reign.

18. For the following successors of Herod the Great, name the regions and dates they ruled and key events in their reigns:

Archelaus; Herod Antipas; Herod Philip; Herod Agrippa I; and Herod Agrippa II.

19. Briefly describe the impact of the following as summarized in the last part of chapter 7: the Greeks; the Romans; and conditions in Palestine.

20. Identify and briefly describe the following resources and their significance: the Apocrypha; the Pseudepigrapha; and the Writings of Josephus.

CHAPTER 8

Jesus and His People

THE NEW TESTAMENT'S MESSAGE is that God sent his Son, Jesus of Nazareth, to complete his plan to save people from the consequences of sin (cf. Acts 3:12-26; 13:16-41; Gal 3:15-4:7; Heb 1:1-2:4; etc.). The New Testament also shows that Jesus' followers, the people who comprise the church, have been commissioned to make known the wisdom of God's eternal purpose to everyone else (cf. Eph 3:8-11). This chapter will survey the last two historical periods of the Bible's story.

13. The Ministry of Jesus
Matthew 1 - Acts 1 (4 BC - 30 AD)

The Amazing Story of Jesus

I am old enough to recall the early days of America's space program in the 1960s. I remember watching launches of some of the Mercury and Gemini missions on live television in the morning before leaving for school. On the afternoon of July 20, 1969, I left our television to tell my father who was busy elsewhere that the Apollo 11 lunar module had set down on the moon. That evening, our family of five were among the millions who watched Neil Armstrong take his first steps on the moon's surface. Throughout the decade of the 1960s, space travel was big news.

As the years passed, however, space travel was relegated to the background. Our country was still sending shuttles, satellites, and other craft into space, but unless something went wrong, the launches and missions were no longer live broadcast events that everyone stopped to watch. The challenge, danger, and achievement were no less real than they had been in the 1960s, but, as a people, we began to take space travel for granted and no longer looked at the events with the same sense of captivated wonder. Space travel had become old news.

Some people experience something similar when they hear the story of Jesus and the beginning of the church. The word "gospel" still means "good news," but the story has been around so long that many see it as old news. Like space travel now, many take Jesus' story for granted.

But stop and think about the story's claims. In the man Jesus, God entered history as a member of the human race (Gal 4:4-5). The infinite and eternal God "became flesh and took up residence among us" (John 1:14; NET). He was a popular teacher whose extraordinarily wise teaching and miraculous deeds astonished people and convinced them that he was the Christ, the Son of God (John 20:30-31). But despite his popularity, the people who had been longing for the coming of God's Messiah turned against him. Their religious leaders handed him over to Pilate, the Roman governor, for execution by crucifixion. When Pilate tried to satisfy them with a lighter punishment, the same people who had cheered Jesus' arrival in Jerusalem days before joined the crowd that shouted, "Crucify him!" And Pilate complied (cf. Matt 21:1-11; 27:20-24).

That was not the end of Jesus' story, however. On the Sunday following his death, God raised him from the dead. During the following forty days he appeared alive to various witnesses, including at least one group that numbered in the hundreds (cf. Acts 1:3, 9-11; 10:36-43; 1 Cor 15:1-11, 20-28). He then ascended to his Father where he was enthroned at his right hand, given all authority in heaven and on earth (John

20:17; Matt 28:18; Acts 1:6-11; Phil 2:9-11). The world had never seen anything like it before. It has never seen anything like it since. *Jesus' story is amazing!*

Those are just the basic facts of his story, however. Its significance is even more astounding. Jesus' death, resurrection, and enthronement were the final acts that completed God's plan to provide humanity the way to be absolved of all the sins they have ever committed or will commit. By living, dying, being raised, and reigning, he makes it possible for all people to be restored to the relationship with God that Adam and Eve once enjoyed in the garden of Eden (see Ephesians 2:1-22). Because of Jesus, people came to see the cross as something precious instead of a cruel and humiliating instrument of torture and death. Because of Jesus, death no longer holds the sense of dread and power over people that it once did. He defeated death and promised that those who follow him will also defeat it (cf. 1 Cor 1:17-18; 2:2, 4-5; 15:20-24, 50-57; 2 Cor 5:19, 21; Rom 8:31-39). *The meaning of Jesus' story is amazing!*

The first Christians were so sure of the truth and meaning of Jesus' story that they ventured to claim that life is futile if Jesus has not been raised (1 Cor 15:17, 19). As Paul of Tarsus declared, "If the dead are not raised, 'Let us eat and drink, for tomorrow we die'" (1 Cor 15:32). The first Christians believed that following Jesus is the only way for people to be reconciled to God (John 14:6; Matt 11:27; Acts 4:12). They lived and died under the conviction that his service, death, resurrection, and enthronement completed God's plan to rescue humanity and that his teaching will be sufficient for all time.

Attention to Details

As amazing as Christianity's claims are, it is possible to recite them in a way that misses what drew people to Jesus and led them to give up everything to follow him. Peter's telling of the story to the Roman centurion named Cornelius helps us begin to fill in the details.

34 So Peter opened his mouth and said: "Truly I understand that God shows no partiality, 35 but in every nation anyone who fears him and does what is right is acceptable to him. 36 As for the word that he sent to Israel, preaching good news of peace through Jesus Christ (he is Lord of all), 37 you yourselves know what happened throughout all Judea, beginning from Galilee after the baptism that John proclaimed: 38 how God anointed Jesus of Nazareth with the Holy Spirit and with power. He went about doing good and healing all who were oppressed by the devil, for God was with him. 39 And we are witnesses of all that he did both in the country of the Jews and in Jerusalem. They put him to death by hanging him on a tree, 40 but God raised him on the third day and made him to appear, 41 not to all the people but to us who had been chosen by God as witnesses, who ate and drank with him after he rose from the dead. 42 And he commanded us to preach to the people and to testify that he is the one appointed by God to be judge of the living and the dead. 43 To him all the prophets bear witness that everyone who believes in him receives forgiveness of sins through his name" (Acts 10:34-43).

In telling Jesus' story, Peter made seven affirmations. (1) Jesus' story began with the preaching of John the Baptist (v. 37). (2) At the appropriate time, God anointed Jesus of Nazareth with the Holy Spirit and power (v. 38). (3) Equipped with the Spirit's power, Jesus went about doing good and healing all who had been oppressed by the devil (v. 38). (4) Despite his exemplary character and all the good he did, Jesus was put to death by crucifixion (v. 39). (5) Death was not the end of his story, however; God raised him from the dead on the third day (v. 40). (6) Following his resurrection, Jesus appeared to chosen witnesses (v. 41). (7) Those witnesses, including Peter, were commissioned to preach to the people and testify that Jesus was the one through whom forgiveness will be granted, just as the prophets had said would happen (vv. 42-43).

When we read the Gospels, we discover that they present Jesus' story in essentially the same way Peter told it to Cornelius. We especially see this when we read Matthew,

Mark, and Luke, the three Gospels that tell Jesus' story from the same perspective. Mark is the shortest and includes the fewest examples of extended accounts of Jesus' teaching. Therefore, we will compare Peter's outline with the way Mark told about Jesus. (1) Jesus' story began with the preaching of John the Baptist (Mark 1:2-8). (2) At the appropriate time, God anointed Jesus of Nazareth with the Holy Spirit and power (Mark 1:9-11; cf. Luke 4:18-21). (3) Equipped with the Spirit's power, Jesus went about doing good and healing all who had been oppressed by the devil (Mark 1:14-10:42). (4) Despite his exemplary character and all the good he did, Jesus was put to death by crucifixion (Mark 14-15). (5) Death was not the end of his story, however; God raised him from the dead on the third day (Mark 16:1-8). (6) Following his resurrection, Jesus appeared to chosen witnesses (Mark 16:9-14cf. Matt 28:1-8, 16-20; Luke 24:1-53; John 20:11-29). (7) Those witnesses were commissioned to preach to the people and testify that Jesus was the one through whom forgiveness will be granted, just as the prophets had said would happen (Mark 16:15-20; cf. Matt 28:16-20; Luke 24:45-49).

In his Gospel, John said that he wrote selectively, choosing to tell about only some of the "signs" Jesus had done. The ones he chose were enough, however, to show that "Jesus is the Christ, the Son of God" (John 20:30-31). Matthew, Mark, and Luke were also selective in their accounts, presenting examples of things Jesus did and said around the Sea of Galilee (Mark 1:16-6:6), in various villages and towns nearby (Mark 6:7-8:26), and in places he went as he resolutely traveled to Jerusalem to complete his God-appointed mission (Luke 9:51-19:44).

Each writer devoted a sizable portion of his writing to Jesus' final debates with various influential Jewish groups and reports of his arrest, trial, crucifixion, and resurrection in Jerusalem (Mark 10:32-16:20; Matt 21:1-28:20; Luke 19:45-24:53; John 12:1-21:25). Each also included material that shows how Jesus' closest followers, the Jewish religious estab-lishment, and the crowds generally were evaluating what he was doing and trying to understand his identity and purpose (Mark 8:27-10:31). Throughout the Gospels, all four writers included details about significant events in Jesus' life, miracles he did, stories (parables) he told, and how he tried to help his closest followers grasp the nature of his mission (see Addition-al Note 1, pp. 122-123).

The Meaning of the Story

In the overview of the Bible's story in chapter 4, we saw that the Gospels and Acts bring out the fact that the ministry, death, and resurrection of Jesus—along with the preaching and service of the early church—completed the story that had be-gun with God's promises to Abraham. The first passage we read in the New Testament traces Jesus' ancestry from Abra-ham to David, from David to Babylon, and then from Babylon to Joseph and Mary (Matt 1:2-17). Luke showed how people saw the events of his birth as the fulfillment of the promises God had made to Israel (Luke 2:25-32). Luke also reported that Jesus connected his baptism and the beginning of his ministry with the Spirit's anointing of the Lord's servant that had been promised in Isaiah (Luke 4:18-21; Isa 61:1-2). In his second volume, Luke included presentations of the gospel by Peter and Paul which show that the church's teaching continued to em-phasize the fulfillment of the promises and completion of the story (Acts 3:11-26; 13:16-41).

To adequately understand the work of Jesus, therefore, we must not see it as an abrupt entrance of God into the world without regard to what had happened before. Instead, it is the climax of the story that God had been working on all along (cf. Eph 3:8-11). Paul emphasized this connection in the opening words of his letter to the Romans where he summarized the "the gospel of God" in terms of the complete story (Rom 1:1-5).

116

First, Paul recalled the origins of the story. He declared that he was preaching what God had "promised beforehand through his prophets in the holy Scriptures" (Rom 1:2). Jesus was the descendant of King David who was to sit on his throne, fulfilling the promise made to David and repeated by the prophets throughout Israel's history (v. 3; cf. 2 Sam 7:12-14; Isa 11; Jer 23:5-6; 33:14-18; Ezek 34:23-31; 37:24-28; Heb 1:5). As the Intertestamental Period ended, the people of Israel were longing intensely for that promise to be fulfilled. Paul's short summary in Romans 1:2-3 reminds us that the good news is not a break with the past, but is the consummation of the story. In other words, Paul declared that the message he preached was *good* news, but it was not *new* news.

Second, Paul said that Jesus was the one who completed the story. He was the designated offspring of Abraham and descendent of David who "was declared to be the Son of God in power according to the Spirit of holiness by his resurrection from the dead" (Rom 1:4). Although brief, the depiction of Jesus' service in verses 2-4 is remarkably comprehensive. He came in the flesh, and was shown to be the anointed one (Messiah or Christ) whom God had promised to send. Although it appeared that his death at the hands of the Jewish and Roman officials showed that his mission had been thwarted, Jesus' ministry was validated by his resurrection.

In fact, the resurrection is the culminating act of the story, reversing the problem created by the entrance of sin and death into the world (Gen 3). In contrast to the insufficient effects of the sacrifices that had been offered previously, Jesus was the perfect offering to atone for human sin (Rom 3:24-26; 2 Cor 5:21; Heb 9:23-10:18). By being raised, he overcame death and the sin that necessarily leads to death (Rom 4:25; 5:18-21; 6:23; 1 Cor 15:50-57). Because God raised Jesus from the dead, those who choose to follow him live as hopeful conquerors over sin and all the trouble it brings into the world (Rom 8:31-39).

14. The Church in Action
Acts 2 - Revelation 22 (30-100 AD)

Paul continued his summary of the story in Romans 1:5-6. He referred to the commission Jesus gave to his followers and the response that is necessary in order to benefit from Jesus' reconciling work. Paul said that he was among those who had "received grace and apostleship." In other words, like all followers of Jesus, he had received forgiveness. And like the twelve who had been Jesus' closest followers during the time of his ministry in Galilee and Judea, he was called to share the news with the world at large. In Paul's words, Jesus' followers had been commissioned "to bring about the obedience of faith for the sake of his name among all the nations, including you who are called to belong to Jesus Christ" (v. 5).

The idea of being called to obedience shows that all people continue to have the freedom to choose whether or not to follow Jesus and serve God. God does *desire* for all people to be saved from sin (1 Tim 2:4; 2 Pet 3:9), but he does not *compel* anyone to follow Jesus who does not choose to do so. All who choose to obey the teaching of Jesus (Matt 28:18; cf. Matt 7:21-23; Luke 6:46; John 8:31-32) are added to his church. Together, they function as a body to show God's wisdom to the nations and continue to build up the church (Eph 3:8-11; 4:11-16; cf. 1 Cor 12:12-31).

The first presentation of Jesus' story after his resurrection and ascension to the Father's right hand shows what the apostles taught was required to become part of his church. In Acts 2, Peter began his address by citing Joel 2:28-32 to show that the amazing events the people observed on Pentecost fulfilled the words of the prophet Joel (Acts 2:17-21). He then referred to the mighty works, wonders, and signs Jesus had done throughout his ministry (v. 22). He told his hearers that they had rejected God's chosen one by handing him over to be crucified, an act that he said was also part of God's plan (v. 23). But, he continued, Jesus' death was not the end of the story.

God had raised him from the dead, a claim Peter supported by referring to Jesus' empty tomb and the testimony of the witnesses to whom he had appeared. This turn of events had also been foreshadowed in the prophetic promises (vv. 24-35). Peter stated the conclusion his hearers needed to accept in verse 36: "Let all the house of Israel therefore know for certain that God has made him both Lord and Christ, this Jesus whom you crucified."

That many of those present that day believed Peter is evident by their response to what he said. "They were cut to the heart, and said to Peter and the rest of the apostles, 'Brothers, what shall we do?'" (v. 37). In that question, the people were acknowledging that Jesus was Lord and Christ and that they were guilty of sin and needed to be forgiven. Speaking in the name of Jesus, Peter told them that if they would "repent and be baptized," they would be forgiven and would "receive the gift of the Holy Spirit" (v. 38). He also said, "For the *promise* is for you and for your children and for all who are far off, everyone whom the Lord our God calls to himself" (v. 39). He went on to expand on his testimony and exhorted them, "Save yourselves from this crooked generation" (v. 40). About three thousand of them were baptized and were added to the group of disciples who had shared the good news with them (v. 41).

Jesus' church had begun. The people who accepted Peter's message were not content to simply enjoy the fact that they were forgiven, however. They devoted themselves to following the apostles' teaching and joined in their works of service (vv. 42-43). They developed a close fellowship in which they "had all things in common" (v. 44). When some among them experienced need, they showed their care for each other by sharing their possessions (v. 45). Together, they attended the temple and shared meals in each other's homes. They showed that they had glad and generous hearts, continued to praise God, and nurtured a good relationship with people who were not part of the church (vv. 46-47). They also joined the apostles in sharing the good news they had received. "And *the Lord added to their number day by day* those who were being saved" (v. 47).

The focus on the believers' devotion to the apostles' teaching in verse 42 is especially important to recall as we think about how the church grew. Wherever the church was planted, its leaders taught new disciples what they needed to know so they could become more mature in their faith (cf. Acts 13:1-3; 1 Cor 12:28; Eph 4:11-12; Col 1:28-29; Heb 5:11-14). When the apostles could not be physically present to teach the new disciples and help them resolve the problems involved in living their faith, they taught them through the written word in epistles (Romans-Jude; cf. especially 1 Thess 2:11-5:11). Sometimes, their teaching was designed to give additional instruction. Sometimes, its purpose was to correct believers who wandered off course and warn them that they needed to get back on track (see Paul's use of the question, "do you not know?" in Rom 6:3, 16; 7:1; 11:2; 1 Cor 3:16; 5:6; 6:2-3, 9, 15-16, 19; 9:13, 24).

Life was often hard for the Christians. Many endured persecution from people who were determined to stop the new faith (cf. Acts 3-5; 8:1-4; 17:1-15; etc.). The last book of the New Testament is "the revelation of Jesus Christ which God gave him" and which was "made known . . . to his servant John" (Rev 1:1). It was written to urge believers to remain loyal to Christ no matter how hard things became (cf. Rev 2:10). Revelation reminded the church that God had delivered his people before, from the oppression by Egypt and Babylon. Likewise, current believers could count on him again. He would reward the faithful followers of Jesus for their loyalty. The Bible's story concludes with a great message of victory and hope.

Conclusion

This completes our survey of the Bible's story. But the story of God's plan to reconcile all humanity to himself, begun and carried out through the promises made to Abraham and fulfilled in Jesus and the church, continues. As we saw above, those who were added to the church were devoted to the teaching of the apostles and committed to continuing the mission Jesus had given to those specially chosen ambassadors. In fact, when the church first began to spread from Jerusalem, it was not the apostles who were scattered, but those whom they had taught. Acts 8:1 says that on the day of Stephen's martyrdom, "a great persecution [arose] against the church in Jerusalem, and they were all scattered throughout the regions of Judea and Samaria, *except the apostles.*" Acts 11:19-20 says that

> those who were scattered because of the persecution that arose over Stephen traveled as far as Phoenicia and Cyprus and Antioch, speaking the word to no one except Jews. But there were some of them, men of Cyprus and Cyrene, who on coming to Antioch spoke to the Hellenists [Greeks] also, preaching the Lord Jesus.

It was the church in Antioch that sent Paul and Barnabas on the first of Paul's missionary journeys (Acts 13:1-3). Paul continued to preach and teach as long as he was free to do so. He told the church in Rome that, after he had delivered a contribution from the mission churches he had established to the believers in Jerusalem, he planned to visit Rome on his way to take the good news west into Spain (Romans 15:22-29). We do not know whether he was ever able to realize his dream. We do know that, when it became clear that his life was near its end, he told Timothy, his apprentice, to continue teaching and to take the necessary steps to "entrust" what he had heard from Paul "to faithful people who will be able to teach others as well" (2 Tim 2:2; NRSV).

We who are now part of Christ's church have benefitted from the teaching that has been handed down from Paul's time to ours. We are the ones who are to continue God's story and tell the good news to the world of our time. No work is more needed or important.

Additional Note 1: Selected Activities of Jesus' Ministry

The books of Matthew, Mark, Luke, and John report the events of Jesus' ministry. The following lists some of his most significant activities. Italics are used to note the climactic events: his trial, crucifixion, resurrection, appearances, and exaltation.

- Prologue: births of John the Baptist and Jesus (Matt 1-2; Luke 1-2).
- Baptism of Jesus (Matt 3:13-17; Mark 1:9-11; Luke 3:21-22).
- Jesus tempted in the wilderness (Matt 4:1-11; Mark 1:12-13; Luke 4:1-13).
- Peter, Andrew, James, and John become Jesus' disciples (Matt 4:18-22; Mark 1:16-20; Luke 5:2-11; John 1:35-42).
- Matthew (Levi) becomes a disciple (Matt 9:9-13; Mark 2:13-17; Luke 5:27-32).
- Jesus chooses the Twelve (Matt 10:2-4; Mark 3:13-19; Luke 6:14-16).
- Jesus tells parables about the kingdom (Matt 13:1-32; Mark 4:1-34; cf. Luke 8:4-15; 13:18-19).
- Jesus calms a storm (Matt 9:28-34; Mark 4:35-41; Luke 8:22-25).
- John the Baptist beheaded by Herod (Matt 14:1-12; Mark 6:14-29; Luke 9:7-9).
- Jesus feeds the 5,000 (Matt 14:13-21; Mark 6:30-44; Luke 9:10-17; John 6:1-14).
- Peter confesses that Jesus is the Christ (Matt 16:13-20; Mark 8:27-30; Luke 9:18-20).
- The Transfiguration of Jesus and appearance with Moses and Elijah (Matt 17:1-13; Mark 9:2-13; Luke 9:28-36).
- Jesus tells the parable of the Good Samaritan (Luke 10:25-37).
- Jesus tells the parable of the rich fool (Luke 12:13-21).
- Jesus tells the parables of the lost sheep, lost coin, and lost boy (prodigal son) (Luke 15:1-32; cf. Matt 18:12-14).
- Jesus heals ten lepers (Luke 17:11-19)
- Jesus tells the parable of the Pharisee and tax collector: who is justified? (Luke 18:9-14).
- Jesus blesses the little children (Matt 19:13-15; Mark 10:13-16; Luke 18:15-17).

- Jesus talks to the rich young man (Matt 19:16-30; Mark 10:17-31; Luke 18:18-30).
- Jesus heals blind Bartimaeus (Matt 20:29-34; Mark 10:46-52; Luke 18:35-43).
- Jesus visits the house of the chief tax collector Zacchaeus (Luke 19:1-10).
- *Jesus enters Jerusalem on a donkey (Matt 21:1-9; Mark 11:1-11; Luke 19:29-38).*
- *Jesus drives the money-changers from the temple (Matt 21:12-22; Mark 11:15-18; Luke 19:45-47; cf. John 2:13-16).*
- *Jesus' authority is questioned (Matt 21:23-46; Mark 11:27-12:12; Luke 20:1-19).*
- *Jesus and the disciples eat the last supper [Passover] (Matt 26:17-30; Mark 14:12-26; Luke 22:7-23).*
- *Jesus predicts Peter's denial (Matt 26:31-35; Mark 14:26-31; Luke 22:31-34; John 13:36-38).*
- *Jesus prays in Gethsemane (Matt 26:36-46; Mark 14:32-42; Luke 22:40-46).*
- *Jesus is betrayed, arrested, and tried by the Sanhedrin (Jewish rulers) (Matt 26:47-68; Mark 14:43-65; Luke 22:47-71; John 18:3-13, 19-24).*
- *Peter denies Jesus (Matt 26:69-75; Mark 14:66-72; Luke 22:56-62; John 18:16-18, 25-27).*
- *Jesus is tried by Pilate (Roman governor) (Matt 27:11-26; Mark 15:1-15; Luke 23:2-25; John 18:29-19:16).*
- *Jesus is crucified (Matt 27:33-61; Mark 15:20-46; Luke 23:33-49; John 19:17-24).*
- *Jesus is buried (Matt 27:57-61; Mark 15:42-47; Luke 23:50-56; John 19:38-42).*
- *Jesus' tomb is found to be empty (Matt 28:1-10; Mark 16:1-8; Luke 24:1-12; John 20:1-10).*
- *Jesus appears to various disciples in different times and places (Matt 28:16-20; Mark 16:9-20; Luke 24:13-53; John 20-21).*
- *Jesus commissions his followers to spread the news about him and offer forgiveness in his name (Matt 28:18-20; Mark 16:15-16; Luke 24:44-49; John 20:21).*

Additional Note 2: Jesus and the Church in History

The lives of Jesus and the earliest Christians took place in history. The people featured in the Bible's story interacted with historical figures who are known to us from other ancient writings. The first believers welcomed investigation into whether the things they claimed had really occurred. In the words of Paul to King Herod Agrippa II, "none of the things" he spoke about with regard to Jesus and his followers would have "escaped [Agrippa's] notice, for *this has not been done in a corner*" (Acts 26:26). In other words, Paul said that the things that had occurred were matters of public record that could be checked and either verified to be true or shown to be false.

Our ability to understand the New Testament is enhanced when we know more about the historical figures and events with which Jesus and the first disciples interacted. The following list highlights key Roman and Jewish rulers and events and takes note of some important examples of Christian people and events intersecting with Roman and Jewish history. It provides a framework for study.

- 27 BC - 14 AD - Augustus is emperor of Rome [Roman]
- ca. 5 BC - Jesus' birth (Luke 1:5; 2:1; Matt 2:1) [Christian]
- 4 BC - Death of Herod the Great, king of the Jews [Jewish]
- 14-37 AD - Tiberius is emperor of Rome [Roman]
- 4-39 AD - Philip Herod (4-34 BC) and Herod Antipas (4-39 BC) rule northern parts of the territory formerly ruled by Herod the Great. [Jewish]
- 18 AD - Caiaphas named Jewish high priest [Jewish]
- 26-36 AD - Pontius Pilate is Roman governor in Judea [Roman, Jewish]
- ca. 26-30 AD - Ministries of John the Baptist and Jesus (Luke 3:1-2) [Christian]
- 37-41 AD - Caligula is emperor of Rome [Roman]
- 37-44 AD - Herod Agrippa I rules the Jews [Jewish]
- 41-54 AD - Claudius is emperor of Rome [Roman]
- ca. 41-44 AD - James, son of Zebedee martyred; Peter imprisoned by Herod Agrippa I (Acts 12:1-19) [Christian]
- 44 AD - Death of Herod Agrippa I (Acts 12:20-23) [Jewish; Christian]

- 44-48 AD - Famine during the reign of Claudius (Acts 11:28) [Roman, Christian]
- 46-47 AD - Judean famine and Paul's relief visit (Acts 11:27-30) [Christian]
- ca. 46-48 AD - Paul's first missionary journey (Acts 13:1-14:28) [Christian]
- 48-70 AD - Herod Agrippa II rules part of Israel [Jewish]
- 49 AD - Claudius expels Jews from the city of Rome because of someone named "Chrestus" (see Acts 18:2) [Roman, Jewish, Christian]
- ca. 49-53 AD - Paul's second missionary journey (Acts 15:36-18:22) [Christian]
- 51-52 AD - Gallio is Roman proconsul of the Greek province of Achaia (Corinth) before whom Paul appeared for judgment (Acts 18:12) [Roman, Christian]
- ca. 53-57 AD - Paul's third missionary journey (Acts 19:1-20:35) [Christian]
- 54-68 AD - Nero is emperor of Rome [Roman]
- 52-59 AD - Felix is Roman governor over Judea [Roman]
- 59-61 AD - Festus is Roman Procurator over Judea [Roman]
- ca. 58-60 AD - Paul arrested in Jerusalem, imprisoned two years in Caesarea (Acts 23:28; 24:27) [Christian]
- ca. 59-60 AD - Paul appeals to Caesar (emperor); Festus decrees that he will be sent to Rome (Acts 25:1, 12) [Christian]
- ca. 60 AD - Paul makes his defense before Herod Agrippa II (Acts 26:1-32) [Christian]
- ca. 60-61 AD - Paul travels to Rome for trial (Acts 27-28) [Christian]
- 62 AD - martyrdom of James, brother of Jesus [Christian]
- ca. 61-63 AD - Paul remains two years under house arrest in Rome (Acts 28:30) [Christian]
- ca. 63-67 - Paul is released from prison and continues his ministry [Christian]
- ca. 64-68 - Arrest and martyrdom of Peter [Christian]
- ca. 67-68 - Paul's second arrest and martyrdom [Christian]
- 81-96 AD - Domitian is emperor of Rome [Roman]
- ca. 90-95 - John banished to the island of Patmos (Rev 1:9) [Christian]

Additional Note 3: The Date of Jesus' Birth

Since the abbreviation BC means "before Christ," why do we say Jesus was born in about 5 BC? The answer requires an understanding of the development of the modern calendar.

The calendar used in the Roman Empire dated events from the establishment of the city of Rome, about 750 years before Jesus was born. In the early sixth century (525 AD) of the Christian era, a monk named Dionysius Exiguus proposed that events be dated from the time of the birth of Jesus. He used the Latin phrase Anno Domini (AD), "in the year of our Lord." The Anno Domini calendar he invented became dominant in western Europe in the ninth and tenth centuries and was incorporated in the Gregorian calendar, the standard civil calendar used since being introduced by Pope Gregory XIII in 1582.[1]

Because Dionysius did not have access to historical data that became available later, his calculations about the date of Herod's death were incorrect. Later analysis determined that Herod the Great had died no later than 4 BC. Since Jesus was born before Herod died (Matt 2:1; Luke 1:5), and Herod did not learn of his birth until sometime afterward (cf. Matt 2:16), scholars calculate that Jesus was born between 6 and 4 BC.

---

[1] In recent years, some authors have replaced BC and AD with the abbreviations BCE ("Before Common Era) and CE ("Common Era"). The numbering of years in both notation systems is the same. The use of BC and AD has a longer history, but the use of BCE and CE can be traced back to the seventeenth century. BCE and CE have been used in recent years as a way to include cultures that do not have a predominantly Christian heritage and out of deference to non-Christians who do not revere Jesus as "Lord" (Domini).

As the summary above indicates, the Anno Domini calendar did not exist until more than 500 years after the birth of Jesus and did not become the dominant notation system in the West until approximately 1,000 years after his birth. Before 525, Christians registered time the same way everyone else in their society did. Since this book is written from a Christian viewpoint, primarily for people who are beginning (or reviewing) their study of the faith, I have used BC and AD. In doing so, I do not intend to imply criticism of any who use or prefer the notations BCE and CE.

For Review and Thought

1. Summarize the "amazing" claims the New Testament makes about what happened in the story of Jesus.

2. What "amazing" results are involved in the meaning of Jesus' story?

3. How convinced were the earliest Christians about the truth and meaning of Jesus' story? What do you think about their conviction?

4. Identify the seven affirmations in Peter's presentation of the story to Cornelius and in Mark's record of Jesus' story.

5. Explain what we mean when we say that the Gospel writers were "selective" in their accounts about Jesus. What do you think about their selectivity?

6. What is the significance of the fact that all of the Gospel writers devoted proportionately more space to the events surrounding Jesus' rejection, death, resurrection, and ascension than to the other astonishing things that he did?

7. What does Romans 1:2-4 show about what the early church understood about how Jesus' story fits with the Bible's whole story?

8. Why is the resurrection of Jesus so important for his ministry? For living today as his followers?

9. Discuss the idea of being called to "obedience" as it relates to being forgiven, God's desire for people to be saved, and for how it fits with the way he created us.

10. Why are Peter's use of Joel 2:28-32 (Acts 2:17-21) and his reference to the "promise" for his hearers and their children important?

11. Explain how the New Testament emphasized the way early Christians were taught and why teaching is important for being loyal believers.

12. In what sense can we say that God's story was completed at the end of the New Testament? In what sense was it not completed?

Final Thoughts and Appendices

Afterword: You Can Do This

IN CHAPTER 2, WE looked at the practical value of getting acquainted with the Bible. The Bible gives us what we need as we learn to follow and live the way of Jesus. It equips us as we face attractions, distractions, and temptations that can push us off course. It teaches us how to live in the midst of alternative lifestyles and competing world views, including multiple religions that make claims for allegiance. Thorough knowledge of the content of the Bible is no substitute for "living a life worthy of the Lord" (Col 1:10; NIV), but it helps us build the necessary foundation for such a life.

The Bible itself shows this. For example, in the early 60s AD when Paul wrote to the church he had planted in Ephesus, he was writing to Christians who were living in a populous city with attractions, distractions, and temptations similar to what we experience. The people around them practiced a very different lifestyle from the one Jesus' followers were called to pursue. They frequented religious centers devoted to as many as fifty gods and goddesses that were worshiped in the city's various temples. Most notable was the temple devoted to the goddess Artemis, included among the seven wonders of the ancient world. Acts 19:35 refers to the belief held by some

Ephesians that the temple housed a "sacred stone that fell from the sky."

In his letter to the Christians in Ephesus, Paul taught them what they needed in order to be loyal to the way of Christ that differed radically from the thinking and lifestyle of the surrounding city (Eph 4:17-6:18; note especially 5:1-11). Before going into detail regarding specific areas of difference, he told them to submit to the instruction of their leaders from whom they would receive teaching that would equip them to loyally follow Christ's way and learn what they needed to contribute to the growth of the church (Eph 4:11-16).

The way Paul wrote indicates that he believed the Ephesians could successfully follow the teaching he gave them, even in the kind of city Ephesus was. They could be distinctive from their neighbors in their honesty, speech, sexual purity, and virtue (Eph 4:25-5:20). Their families and the way they responded to those with power over them could be exemplary models of commitment, decorum, and diligence (5:21-6:9). They could learn to see through the false narratives of their culture and "be strong in the Lord" (6:10-18).

As your knowledge of the Bible grows, so will your strength to live a life worthy of the Lord. Here are some basic things to keep in mind as you go forward and continue your study.

First, always remember three fundamental truths about the Bible's nature, story, and value. It is the revelation of God's will for how to live (cf. 2 Pet 1:3-4; Jude 3). Its story culminates in the New Testament with Jesus' example and authoritative teaching (cf. Matt 16:19; John 14:26; 16:12; 1 Cor 2:9-13; Eph 3:4-5; Gal 1:6-11; Col 3:17). It has the power to change your life and prepare you for every good work (2 Tim 3:17; cf. Heb 4:12; Rom 12:2; Psa 119:130, 149; Rom 1:16).

But as vital as these truths are, for practical use, it is equally if not more important to remember that God wants you to *understand* the Bible. Passages in both Testaments confirm this. When the people of Israel returned from exile, Ezra the scribe gathered them together to hear the reading of God's word so they would understand what it said (Ezra 7:10; Neh 8:1-8). Paul told the Ephesians that when they read his letter, they could "perceive [his] insight into the mystery of Christ" that had been revealed to him (Eph 3:3-4). He added that his goal in his teaching and writing was "to bring to light for *everyone* what is the plan of the mystery hidden for ages in God . . ." (v. 9). Similarly, Peter told his readers to have a desire for God's word that was like the longing a new baby has for milk so they could "grow up into salvation" (1 Pet 2:2).

To make sure people could understand it, the Bible was written in the languages and styles that were common among average people in everyday life, not the styles of the highly educated and elite. God wanted everyone to understand the language of the Bible.

Are there concepts in the Bible that stretch our thinking and are more difficult to understand? Yes. Since the Bible is revealing aspects of God's nature and mind (Rom 11:33-36; 1 Cor 2:9-13), we expect as much. The Bible itself is candid about the challenge. Peter, for example, said that some things in Paul's writings were hard to understand. He did not, however, say they were impossible to understand, but that they were being misunderstood because they were being "twisted" (2 Pet 3:15-16).

As you continue to study the Bible, you should take comfort in the fact that God wants you to understand. Rely on that assurance and apply yourself, confident that, as you study, you *can* understand, you *can* learn more, and you *can* go deeper into his knowledge.

Keep studying.

Appendix 1: Bible Study Resources

NUMEROUS POPULAR LEVEL RESOURCES are available to aid our understanding of the Bible. The following will be useful to begin building a study library.

General Introductions to the Bible

Michael C. Armour. *A Newcomer's Guide to the Bible: Themes and Timelines.* Joplin, MO: College Press Publishing, 1999.

Gordon D. Fee and Douglas Stuart. *How To Read the Bible Book by Book: A Guided Tour.* Grand Rapids, MI: Zondervan, 2002.

_____, *How to Read the Bible for All Its Worth*, 4th ed. Grand Rapids, MI: Zondervan, 2014.

Bible Dictionaries

David Noel Freedman, ed. *Eerdmans Dictionary of the Bible.* Grand Rapids, MI: William B. Eerdmans Publishing Company, 2000.

D. R. W. Wood, ed. *New Bible Dictionary.* Downer's Grove, IL: InterVarsity Press, 1996.

Introductions to the Bible's Teaching

F. F. Bruce. *The Message of the New Testament.* Grand Rapids, MI: William B. Eerdmans Publishing Company, 1973.

H. L. Ellison. *The Message of the Old Testament.* Eugene, OR: Wipf and Stock Publishers, 2004.

Bible Atlas

John D. Currid and David P. Barrett. *Crossway ESV Bible Atlas.* Wheaton, IL: Crossway, 2010.

Background Charts and Chronologies

H. Wayne House. *Chronological and Background Charts of The New Testament.* 2nd ed. Grand Rapids, MI: Zondervan, 2009.

Marsha A. Ellis Smith, ed. *Holman Book of Biblical Charts, Maps, and Reconstructions.* Nashville, TN: Broadman & Holman Publishers, 1993.

John H. Walton. *Chronological and Background Charts of the Old Testament.* rev. ed. Grand Rapids, MI: Zondervan, 1994.

Software and Websites

Technology allows easy access to multiple resources. As I write this, for example, I can use the Bible Gateway website to look up passages in fifty-nine English translations.[1] Software programs, mobile apps, and websites enable us to consult ancient historical sources, atlases, Bible commentaries, and so on. Hebrew and Greek texts and related tools are also available. Libraries of information are accessible in a matter of seconds. As with all study resources, and the internet generally, these materials should be read critically and compared with other sources and sites known for their scholarly competence.

That said, it is a wonderful time to be a Bible student!

---

[1] https://www.biblegateway.com/versions/. Accessed March 5, 2019.

Appendix 2: Learning the Books of the Bible

Activities for Teaching the Books of the Bible

AFTER COVERING CHAPTER 1, "What Is the Bible?" teachers may follow up with a class (or as an activity within a class session) that does one or more of the following.

1. Work through *a books of the Bible test* (divisions matching, books before and after sections; see below). Run copies for students, but let the class work through the test together by using presentation slides or a transparency. An example has been included below for your use, or you may develop your own.

2. *Books of the Bible Drill.* Secure a foam ball that students can safely toss to one another. To begin, say a book of the Bible yourself, or give the ball to a student to begin. Whoever begins then tosses the ball to another student who tosses it to a third student, and so on (randomly) around the room. Each student who receives the ball says the next book in the order. (Note: if a teacher notices that some students are being skipped, vary the exercise by asking each student to toss the ball back to the teacher who can then randomly select students and include everyone.)

3. *Sword Drill* (see Ephesians 6:17). Depending on the size of the class, select a group (or do with the class as a whole) and have students sit with their Bibles closed on their laps. Call out a Bible reference and ask the first student who successfully finds the verse to read it. This is a practical test of knowing the order of the books. (Alternately: if a class is larger, divide it into teams, and see which team can score the most points from a series of references. Be sure to organize the competition so that [a] each student participates, and [b] teams are divided evenly for a fairer competition. Consider giving some small prize for the team with the most points.)

These activities can be repeated and alternated from week-to-week at the beginning or end of class to review the books. It will be good to review even as you are completing subsequent lessons in this series.

Books of the Bible Test

Check your knowledge of the books and divisions of the Bible with the following test.

I. MATCHING. Match the book of the Bible to the division in which it appears by writing the letter that corresponds to the division in the blank beside each book.

a. Law   f. Gospels

b. OT History   g. NT History

c. Poetry   h. Paul's Epistles

d. OT - Major Prophets   i. General Epistles

e. OT - Minor Prophets   j. NT Prophets

___ Exodus   ___ Nehemiah

___ 2 Kings   ___ Ecclesiastes

___ Romans   ___ Amos

___ Deuteronomy   ___ Philemon

___ 1 Thessalonians   ___ Proverbs

___ Jonah   ___ Ruth

___ 2 Corinthians   ___ Esther

___ Nahum   ___ Acts

___ Mark   ___ Zechariah

___ Jeremiah   ___ 1 Chronicles

___ Titus   ___ Revelation

___ Joel   ___ Daniel

___ 2 Timothy   ___ 1 Peter

___ Hebrews   ___ Judges

___ John   ___ 3 John

___ Numbers   ___ Job

II. BIBLE BOOKS. For each book listed, write the books that
are listed before (left) and after (right).

	Numbers	
_____	Ephesians	_____
_____	Psalms	_____
_____	1 John	_____
_____	Joshua	_____
_____	Ruth	_____
_____	Romans	_____
_____	Malachi	_____
_____	Galatians	_____
_____	Leviticus	_____
_____	Zephaniah	_____
_____	Jeremiah	_____
_____	Ezra	_____
_____	Hosea	_____
_____	2 Corinthians	_____
_____	Micah	_____
_____	Daniel	_____
_____	Philippians	_____
_____	Acts	_____
_____	Jude	_____
_____	Judges	_____
_____	1 Timothy	_____
_____	Matthew	_____
_____	2 Timothy	_____

Acknowledgments

THE LIST OF PEOPLE to whom I am indebted for this project begins with my parents, Ralph and Irma Anguish, who always modeled lives of faith and influenced my early belief. They also allowed me to question, investigate, and develop a faith of my own, not one I merely inherited.

Encouragement, questions to pursue, and invaluable insights also came from teachers and students—in both church and school settings—as well as mentors, colleagues in ministry and education, and others with whom I have had many enriching discussions on a variety of subjects.

Important suggestions for changes to early drafts came from family and friends whom I invited to read the book. My daughter-in-law, Amy, took time from revisions on her second book—not to mention her reading time while my grandchildren were napping—to edit the manuscript and offer other suggestions for completing and spreading the word about this book. My sons, Jeremy and Nathan, read from their history-teacher perspectives, along with keen eyes for better word and phrasing choices.

David Parker, a friend whose professional training is Geography and Environmental Engineering and is one of the best Bible students I know, pointed out several places where the points I intended could be better made or would we better received. Dr. Harold Redd, minister of both the Midtown and Raleigh Springs churches of Christ in Memphis, and a first-rate Bible scholar, also read the book and offered encouragement. Kenneth Mills designed the cover and made helpful suggestions for improving its content and appeal. His passion for the way of the Lord and growth of his people is inspiring.

Of course, none of these good people are accountable for any errors of fact, detail, or style that remain. That responsibility is mine alone.

Cancer took my wife Carlynn from us in 2017. Had she lived, she would have shared numerous wise insights and important suggestions that would have helped every facet of this project. I'm sure of that because that's what she consistently did throughout our nearly forty years of married life. She was my closest friend and biggest booster. She also made it easier for me to focus on the study and work necessary to finish tasks like this. I miss her greatly.

Carlynn had an insatiable desire to pursue Berea-like Bible study and pass on a thoughtful faith to children. I have no doubt she would have continued her study and been quite passionate about encouraging her grandchildren to grow their own faith. I dedicate this volume to her memory with the hope that it will be true to her desire to understand Scripture and contribute to her dream of passing on the faith to her grandchildren and other eager learners.

"But grow in the grace and knowledge of our Lord and Savior Jesus Christ. To him be the glory both now and to the day of eternity. Amen" (2 Peter 3:18).

CPSIA information can be obtained
at www.ICGtesting.com
Printed in the USA
FFHW010926120519
52412208-57818FF

9 780578 434